CURRICULUM BASED ASSESSMENT

Third Edition

CURRICULUM BASED ASSESSMENT

A Primer

By

CHARLES H. HARGIS

Professor
College of Education, Health and Human Sciences
The University of Tennessee
Knoxville, Tennessee

CHARLES C THOMAS • PUBLISHER, LTD.
Springfield • Illinois • U.S.A.

Published and Distributed Throughout the World by

CHARLES C THOMAS • PUBLISHER, LTD.
2600 South First Street
Springfield, Illinois 62704

©2005 by CHARLES C THOMAS • PUBLISHER, LTD.

ISBN 0-398-07552-2 (paper)

Library of Congress Catalog Card Number: 2004058055

Printed in the United States of America
CR-R-3

Library of Congress Cataloging-in-Publication Data

Hargis, Charles H.
    Curriculum based assessment : a primer / by Charles H. Hargis
3rd ed.
        p. cm.
    Includes bibliographical references and Index
    ISBN 0-398-07552-2 (pbk.)
    1. Cirruculum-based assessment--United States. 2. Educational
tests and measurements--United States. 3. Learning disabled chil-
dren--Education--United States. I. Title.

LB3060.32.C74H37 2004
371.2'7--dc22

                                                              2004058055

PREFACE

In the first edition, I attempted to explain the concepts that make up, what I called curriculum-based assessment. I provided some illustrations on its use and made some suggestions on its implementation.

The ingredients of this curriculum-based assessment were not new. I relied heavily on work done by Arthur Gates and Emmett Betts generations ago. The ideas I expressed were not new or at all complex. Yet, the results of the recipe that synthesized its components were novel and, on some points, controversial. Still, I remain convinced it represents the best way for low achieving and learning disabled students to gain adequate educational opportunity. The principles have proven sound and, when applied, benefit all children. The additions to this edition are in the way of providing detail and explanation in the context of current and emerging issues in educational assessment and standards.

Academics typically prefer to deal with arcane and obscure sources of our educational ills. They do not like to believe that our problems may be due to such obvious, and to them trivial, causes, certainly not if it would implicate them as part of the problem. But, as Justice Holmes believed, it is the obvious that generally needs explanation. I have again further attempted to explain the obvious in this third edition.

C.H.H.

CONTENTS

CURRICULUM BASED ASSESSMENT

Chapter 1

CENTRAL CONCEPTS

The Bed of Procrustes

Remember Procrustes? He was that legendary scoundrel from Attica with that horrible iron bed. Travelers who were unfortunate enough to sleep in it were either stretched to fit with a rack if too short or were shortened with an ax if too tall.

Fortunately, Theseus took care of Procrustes and his bed. Unfortunately, there is still a Procrustean bed to which a group of children must fit.

This iron bed is the typical curriculum for kindergarten through high school. Routinely, student progress is measured against the curricular components of her or his particular grade. Each grade has a set of curricular objectives for each subject sequenced over the nine-month school year. The assessment procedures in use determine how the student measures up to the curricular objectives. If the student doesn't measure up, then she or he is given a failing grade. Regular failure will attract a label, usually suggesting a learning disability. Indeed, failure is the primary diagnostic procedure by which we identify learning disabled children.

Procrustes now is the school board, the administration, and the teachers who design and control the curricular beds to which they force children to fit. The axes and racks now used to fit students to these iron curricular beds are the traditional forms of assessment used to assign failure when students don't measure up. Fifteen to twenty-five percent of all students don't fit; consequently they fail.

Despite substantial learning ability, these students, who are often called learning disabled, are actually casualties of inflexible curricula.

There needs to be a modern Theseus come to slay this new Procrustes and replace his iron bed with one more generous and humane. Curriculum-based assessment (CBA) is such a champion. It is a system used to adjust the curriculum to fit students and so eliminate such unfortunate casualties.

An Early Observation

The observation that the curriculum is rigid is not new. As early as 1899 William J. Shearer noted that not all students of an age fitted their grade very well (Shearer, 1899). William Hawley Smith (1912) described the great attrition rate in America's schools that he felt was directly attributable to rigid curricular organization. Emmett Betts (1936) stated that many reading problems were created simply because we do not make basic adjustments to deal with individual differences. Betts estimated at the time that about 15 percent of the children were reading disabled in this way. Later (1946) he elaborated on the problem, attributing it also to the "lock step" nature of school organization. Here instruction was provided based on the assumption that every child was to climb the same curriculum ladder. Objectives were set up in grade levels. Each level represented a rung on the curricular ladder. At about the same chronological age, usually 6, children took the first step, the first grade. The goal of each teacher was to prepare the class for the next grade. The grade itself was broken into units of work through which all children were to proceed. Reading programs and content areas alike were designed for these gradations or steps on the assumption that all children are capable of uniform achievement. Children who could not manage to maintain this rate of achievement might be provided with "remedial" instruction to help them achieve grade level. Those who could not keep the pace were either socially promoted or repeated the grade. The same rate of learning progress was required of all children regardless of the individual intrinsic readiness level or speed of learning.

Much verbiage has been devoted to the importance of individual differences in instruction. However, in practice the comments of Betts apply quite accurately to today's schools.

George Spache (1976) said that flexible, primary-level teachers can handle students that vary six months or so from exact grade placement. However, in the existing structure a child who functions a year or more below grade placement presents a demand for individualized instruction that the average teacher does not recognize or readily meet. Spache also pointed out that 30 percent of students above the primary grades are a year or more below grade-level placement in reading achievement.

Harris and Sipay (1975) stated that 25 percent of all students need reading instruction that differs from regular reading programs. These "slow learners" require materials that proceed at a slower pace. Frank Smith (2001) stated that the way our educational system structures time produces many of our learning casualties. Many students require substantially more time to learn than is allowed in our lock-step school organization. He believes that it is time to take a radical new look at an organizational system that is about 150 years old, introduced about the same time that technology of industrial efficiency was introducing the production line. This was the model that our emerging free public schools chose to adopt and remains in place.

Jansky and de Hirsch (1972) showed that teachers rated as adequate by their principals had a failure rate of 23 percent of their students. However, teachers rated as poor showed a 49 percent student failure rate. The Cooperative Research

Program in First-Grade Reading Instruction (Bond and Dykstra, 1967/1997) forcefully confirmed the importance of a good teacher in learning, regardless of method of reading instruction. These data strongly indicate that teachers influence the effectiveness of reading instruction, but it is also apparent that without a major adjustment in the management of the curriculum itself, many so-called learning disabled children will continue to be products or casualties of rigid curricular structures.

Testing for Teaching

Most tests in use today have little value in providing specific information on where students are on the scope-and-sequence of skills that make up any curricular area. However, it is precisely this information that is necessary for planning instruction for individual students. Teaching must be begun at a level of readiness that permits students to succeed. As Richard Stiggins (2002) points out most testing is not done **for** learning; it is done of learning. Standards are set for schools, schools systems, or teachers. These standards or objectives are set by grade and subject level. When assessment is done in this way it does not tell specifically where students are on a curricular hierarchy. For students who are functioning either below or above grade level, it does not show what they have learned and what they need to learn next. I have likened this type of assessment to a map with no landmark to show where you are (Hargis, 2003). It is like a map of stores at a mall in which the "You are here" marker has been removed. Instruction cannot successfully proceed with individual students without this information.

Curriculum-based assessment is designed to insure that there is a correspondence between the tests and testing procedures the scope-and-sequence skills on the curriculum in use. This correspondence is necessary not only for test validity but to place low achieving and learning disabled students at a place on the curriculum where they can work success-fully and make progress.

Much informal testing that goes on in classrooms today is for the purpose of assigning grades. When testing is done this way, low achieving and learning disabled student continue to get poor and failing grades. This remains their unfortunate lot in most classrooms. This is how they are identified. The focus of assessment must change for these children. The test-ing procedures should not be used to assign grades but to accurately assign a student to a level of instruction where he or she can succeed and achieve. Success is fundamental to CBA.

Success and Achievement

Success is certainly more than just avoiding failure, and throughout the book, more precise definitions of success in various instructional situations will be added. Fundamental-ly, success can be viewed as what is needed to keep a student on task to the satisfactory completion of an instruction activ-ity. If a task is too difficult, a student cannot remain on task. If a task is too difficult, a student cannot pursue it to a satis-factory end. Achievement is tied to amount of time spent on learning. Time off task is not time engaged in learning. CBA is intended to identify tasks and activities that are doable for individual students; activities and objectives that are an appropriate level of difficulty so that these students can be rewarded by success experiences and so that they can remain on-task to completion.

There is an old saying that applies to the objective of CBA. It is: "The more you do; the more you can do." We should also add, "Success breeds success." Success and learning time go together. Doing and succeeding produce achievement. Doing and succeeding are necessary benefits of curriculum-based assessment and instruction. They are necessary if chil-dren are to achieve to their potential.

Curing Individual Differences

All too often individual differences in learning ability are unwittingly viewed as curable maladies. However, our attempts to cure them produce more casualties. We make the misguided attempt to force all children to perform up to, or down to, grade level standards. A quarter typically and unfortunately fail. The actual range of academic capability or readiness in typical first grade classrooms exceeds two and one-half years. As this group moves up through each grade, the achievement range increases by more than one year each succeeding year. By the end of the sixth grade the range will be about eight years. By the time they reach ninth grade, a quarter of the students will have a reading level below the seventh level. However, a quarter of them will be reading well above the tenth grade level (Hargis, 1999). This widening range should be viewed as being as normal as the expected differences in height, motor-skill development, artistic or musical talent, etc. CBA is intended to provide a means for accepting and working with the range of readiness levels and learning rates that always exist.

Programming for Success

Programming for success in the face of such a great range of individual differences can be intimidating. However, living with the consequences of not programming for the success of children with these differences often is demoralizing. There is nothing more dear to the heart of a teacher than having children on-task and successfully completing their assignments.

Children who are failing and have little work that they can do or complete, demonstrate other behaviors that contribute to the demoralization. The children will be off-task in a variety of ways, some of which are disruptive or annoying. Chronic failure will attack and then erode the child's self-concept. This state produces still more negative behavioral consequences. In fact, much of the negative behavior associated with learning disabled children is attributable to chronic failure and frustration.

Dealing with individual differences effectively is very hard work. However, dealing with the consequences of not doing so is really harder. CBA is a technique developed to help teachers deal effectively with individual differences.

The learning problems of all learning disabled children are not necessarily simply the result of a mismatch between their ability and curricular demands. There is a small percentage of students who are labeled as learning disabled whose learning problems are caused to greater of lesser extent by central nervous system abnormality. There are also some whose problems are the result of nutritional or metabolic disorders. Social factors contribute in some instances as well. CBA directly addresses these problems, and methods of attending to them will be considered later in the book. Especially with these children, however, matching the curriculum to the individual is of primary importance.

Chapter 2

SUCCESS OR CHALLENGE

A Double Standard

Why is it that we think that low achieving students are not challenged enough? When students lag behind grade level standards, they do so because they lack challenge; or so the prevailing view suggests. "They'll never learn if they're not challenged," is an often-heard expression in regard to low achieving students. However, the reverse is true. These students fall behind because they are challenged beyond their capacity to engage in learning successfully. And, as Forell (1985) pointed out so well, the history of higher achieving students has been one of success and of being comfortably fitted to their instructional materials. While, on the other hand, low achievers are frequently challenged with materials above their skill level.

Success is fully evident in the performance of higher achieving students. In reading groups they read easily and fluently. They encounter few unknown words. Their comprehension is high. In arithmetic and other content areas, the same evidence appears as well. Their performance is marked by comfortable success.

It should be obvious that this level of success is important for achievement. Low achieving students deserve the same standard as the high achieving ones. Low achievers need a comfortable placement on the curricular path in order to achieve to their potential. Remember, success is fundamental to achievement. Lack of success hampers achievement.

The double standard should be eliminated. This criterion of success needs to be used for all students.

Why We Require Failure

If success is so important a factor in achievement, why do we require so much failure? Tradition may be one answer; that's the way we've always done it. And, as Santayana stated, "Habit is stronger than reason." Another likely answer is that teachers are misled by the success of the majority of their students. If so many students do so well, certainly the rest of them could if they really tried. Teachers have a powerful need to have all students working at grade level. Using grade level materials gives the appearance of working at grade level, even if the student is failing. That is the way the curriculum is structured and that is the way commercial instructional material is structured as well. These are strong factors affecting the expectations we have for students in each chronological age group.

Other reasons have to do with the maintenance of "standards." This notion assumes that some students always fail. After all, isn't that why we have grades? A related argument is that giving lower grades makes it more important to work harder. Students who are doing poorly haven't been challenged enough.

We must break from the practice of requiring failure. Low achieving students are challenged far too much. The double standard must be abandoned. Failure produces no increase in achievement. It is inhumane. We should not compel primary age children to endure continued frustration and failure. There are no benefits.

Why Failure Fails

Failure precludes the conditions necessary for achievement. The harder an instructional activity is for a student, the slower and more painstaking is the student's progress through it. In reading selections, he or she will struggle with word identification of many unfamiliar words. Too many new words mean there are insufficient familiar words to aid in the identification of the unfamiliar ones. Without this effective use of context not only does word identification suffer, comprehension suffers as well. And finally, when it is too hard, the student cannot maintain her or his attention on the reading task. The student simply cannot do it. When students reach this frustrating level, they are no longer actively engaged in the activity. Learning time is limited or eliminated entirely. Yet, engaged learning time is necessary for achievement. This is true for all instructional areas.

The student is also missing two additional important benefits of appropriately matched instructional materials. These two benefits are success and the reward gained from completing a task. These two benefits are enormously encouraging to a student (Hargis, 1982).

Continued failure produces a wide range of negative behaviors in children. At the daily activity level, tasks that are too difficult cannot maintain a student's attention. Students will very shortly be off-task if they can't do the assignment. The range of off-task behavior will range from quiet day dreaming to annoying disturbances. This requires nonproductive teacher attention.

Continued failure often erodes the self-concept and self-confidence of children. This can have further compounding behavioral effects. Learned Helplessness (Grimes, 1981) is a condition where some children lower their expectations of future success and avoid tasks. This condition occurs in some children faced with an imbalance of negative feedback and failure. The less children experience success, the more avoidance behavior they will have. This is a further compounding effect. Children who need more time on task will be learning to avoid the task.

Success

We must learn from our successes and our failures. Success does breed success. Continued failure does foster failure. Children will not willingly or voluntarily fail; failure is imposed.

An overlooked principle of learning is that success is its main ingredient. If a student gets the right answer to a problem enough times they will learn to that kind of problem correctly. The condition for getting the answers successfully must be set up for each and every student. These conditions are missing for too many of our students.

Stanovich (1986) described the effects of success in regard to learning to read. He attributed good achievement in learning to read as "Matthew effects." Good achievement described the "rich-get-richer" side of Matthew effects. The "poor-get-poorer" side described what happened to student who experienced little or no success.

The concept of Matthew effects comes from the Bible in the Gospel according to Saint Matthew:

> For whosoever hath, to him shall be given, and he shall have more abundance: but whosoever hath not, from him shall be taken away even that he hath. (XIII:12)

> For unto everyone that hath shall be given, and he shall have abundance: but from him that hath not shall be taken away even that which he hath. (XXV:29)

Stanovich suggested that the children who are reading well and who have good vocabularies will read more, learn more word meanings through the many opportunities they have for reading in other subject areas and incidental encounters with print. Consequently, they learn to read even better. However, when students are failing these opportunities don't exist. They then fall farther and farther behind.

Success optimizes achievement. We must abandon the notion of achievement to grade level standards. We must aim for achievement to the capacity of each student. This can only be reached by insuring that each child experiences success in the same measure as his higher achieving peer. When this occurs, the curriculum casualty will be eliminated from the list of learning disabilities.

If success is planned, then time on-task can occur. Behavior is modified. Instruction, instead of problem off-task behavior, can then become the focus of the teacher's efforts. The student and teacher enter a positive cycle of success and achievement. The child gains in self-concept and confidence. Children who are increasingly on-task and completing assignments are a joy to any teacher. Real achievement occurs and the quality of instruction appears to be better, and it is.

Forell (1985) reported a change in her low achieving group of students from the 23rd percentile to the 48th on the Iowa Tests of Basic Skills after a reading program emphasizing success was implemented. Improvements in scores of the extremes of any population have a large effect on the mean scores for the group of which they are a part. It is a wise policy to insure the success of the low achieving group. Not only does it benefit the students, but it makes their teacher look good.

The Objective of CBA

The primary objective of CBA is the success of students. There are two assessment steps in achieving this end and much of the book will be devoted to their details. The first step is finding a level on the curriculum where the student can succeed. Sometimes this is difficult, but the assessment methods are simple and straight-forward. The second step is incorporating assessment practices in the daily teaching activities so that success is an ongoing affair. Assessment will become the intimate companion of instruction; and, in fact, it should become an intrinsic part of instruction.

Since success becomes the primary objective under CBA, the focus of assessment practice must change to what skills a child has. Success and achievement must be built on what the child can do. Almost any test learning disabled and low achieving children get will show a multitude of deficits, but it is more important to identify strengths.

CBA must also provide detailed directions on the preparation and identification of appropriate instructional material which produce the success objective. Here, the assessment procedure checks student performance and the adequacy of the instructional activities and materials simultaneously. This dimension of assessment will be considered in some detail later.

Whose Fault?

Often, when a child fails or does poorly in school we assume that the cause is within the child. We begin to look for evidence of a disability. The most trivial behavioral evidence may be used to find a label for the child. If this evidence happens to be lacking, the child may simply be labeled as lazy.

When children are blamed, particularly if they are considered slow or lazy, they may have the added pain of punishment. The following incident illustrates such an instance in the case of two fifth-grade boys who were kept in from recess to complete work they had not finished in class: Looking over the uncompleted seatwork, it was apparent that it was considerably too difficult for either boy. Their responses were mostly errors, and they seemed to be mainly random guessing. However, the reaction and attitude of the two boys was contrasting. One boy was inured and somewhat surly. He slouched in his seat and drummed his pencil on the desk top. He was making no attempt to finish his work. He looked disdainfully at his teary-eyed companion who was moving his paper and pencil fitfully over his desk top, hoping, possibly, that a different perspective might miraculously make the work doable. Then the first boy said to the distraught one, "I can sit here till the bus leaves. It doesn't bother me." He had hardened himself to the discomfort of the loss of free time at school. He knew that the school bus would always come to rescue him. I couldn't help feeling admiration for the boy's durability. He had learned to cope with failure. On the other hand, I couldn't help but feel sympathy for the other child. The anxiety affect of failure was quite evident in his manner. Both of these children deserve fairer treatment. How different their circumstances would be if the curriculum had been adjusted to fit them.

If there is blame to be placed, it should be on the lack of assessment procedures that sensitively place children on instructional pathways where failure does not result. When children are permitted to work where they should, they normally succeed, and unfortunate situations like those illustrated above do not occur.

The Same Scores

The notion that all children must succeed by design has a novel effect. If success is planned, it means that all children will demonstrate roughly the same response levels in the work they do. High scores indicate success. The result of a good match between instructional material and student is a high level of performance.

Think of the system as basically the reverse of standard practice. In most classrooms, the students are given the standard instructional material on the same place in the curricular ladder. The children always vary in readiness and ability, so we expect some students to do very well and others to do poorly. When curriculum-based assessment is used, the instructional material must be varied to produce similar scores in all children. Curriculum-based assessment co varies instruction with student skill level. "Standard practice" imposes the same grade level material on variable student, thus producing variable scores.

Scores, when using CBA, should appear in the narrow band that indicates the student is on-task, engaged in learning and succeeding. Only a fairly narrow performance band is acceptable.

Varying instructional level, not scores, is fundamental to CBA.

Answering Skeptics

Certain comments and questions arise when these notions are presented. "How can a classroom teacher, with 25 to 30 students, manage this?" "It sounds good, but it would cost too much money."

The answer to these questions is that teachers have provided and continue to provide, students functioning at several different grade levels in one classroom with appropriately differentiated instruction. This is an essential practice for a good teacher. Also, thousands of children are taught in small rural schools where a single teacher serves more than one grade level at once. One still finds classrooms that are made up of all the primary grades or the intermediate grades or the middle school grades. There are still some hundreds of schools with one teacher for all twelve grades, and many high schools with graduating classes of under a dozen. Here, teachers routinely manage many levels and subjects, and, I should add that they often do it quite well.

Dealing with many different levels of instruction in one room is simply a matter of your expectation. In multi-graded classrooms, one expects to deal with quite different levels of instruction, so it is done. In single-grade classrooms, we think we have reduced the student variation, but we haven't. The actual instructional levels of the students always cover several years. Teachers should expect to provide instruction at these different levels. It requires different organizational practices, but a great many teachers already manage to do this as if it were commonplace routine.

As to the comment concerning money, the cost should be no different than for the operation of any other classroom with the same number of students in that school system. The curricular materials that are already available will need redistribution so that a variety of levels will be available in each classroom, but no new material is needed.

Remember; teachers deal with the differences in their classroom one-way-or-the-other, like-it-or-not. It seems it would be far better for teachers to deal with problems of variable instruction than to deal with the off-task behavior and lack of achievement.

Chapter 3

ASSESSMENT THAT IS
CURRICULUM BASED

With this form of CBA, Assessment is used for preventing failure and programming success. To do this, it must provide direct guidance in planning daily instructional activities. As its name shows, assessment should be drawn from the curriculum that is the basis for instruction. All too often tests exist quite independently from the curriculum being used. These tests are of no direct help in meeting the daily curricular/instructional demands place on teachers and students. Tests that are not curriculum based often are wasted effort, and the worst have negative effects. Tests that have relevance to teachers and students speak to the substantive demands of daily instruction and materials preparation, and so are curriculum based.

Curriculum is assigned to grade levels. This is an obstacle to using curriculum-based assessment. If curriculum-based assessment is to be used well, a curriculum should be laid out on a seamless continuum. The scope and sequence of skills or objectives should be borderless. It should be sequenced by order of difficulty and by readiness relationships. As curricula are now organized, a quarter of the students in each grade will need to be engaged in learning activities on the curriculum that are well below the items that are assigned to that grade. And a quarter of the students in each grade will be capable of performing in curricular activities that are well above their grade placement. Curriculum-based assessment is used to find the correct place on a curriculum scope and sequence that will permit student success. This means that assessment must find a place on the curriculum that will be well above or well below the grade placement of about half the students in every grade. To do this adequately challenges the credibility of the lock-step organization of our schools. More will be said about this later, but first is a discussion of basic assessment terms.

Some Assessment Terms

A later chapter focuses entirely on validity and reliability, but for now a brief description is in order.

Validity is the most important quality of a test. A valid test measures exactly what you want to measure and nothing else. So, the most important type of validity is content validity. Tests should relate with precision to what is being taught. Tests that do this have content validity. Content validity is the required form of validity for curriculum-based assessment. In order for a test to have content validity, the test should be made up of a sufficient number of items from the curricular area being measured. A test with an adequate representation of such items can accurately measure the level of achievement in that particular area.

The validity of some tests is determined by comparing it with established instruments that are used to measure the same things. This type of validity is called criterion-related validity. This form of validity assumes that the established instrument is itself valid. At any rate, this form of validity in no way assures that the test has a sufficient representation of items concerning the area being measured to give it content validity. Many standard diagnostic and achievement tests bear more resemblance to other tests than they do to the content of the curriculum they are used with. Jenkins and Pany (1978) studied standardized reading tests and found that they did not representatively sample the content of different reading curricula. Current general achievement tests are receiving criticism because they contain too many items that assess mastery of content that is not being taught. Significant biases exist that in turn suggest that student achievement in a particular curriculum may not be reflected in achievement test scores.

Standards, the pressure on schools to have high standards, first affect the content of achievement tests. We want to see if the standards are achieved so the standards measures appear as content on achievement tests. The standards may not as yet be incorporated in the curriculum. The tests are measuring content that is not as yet being taught; content validity is missing from these tests. Students do poorly and everyone is unhappy.

The content from one reading curriculum to another varies substantially. This is also true of mathematics, social studies, and science curricula. It is unlikely that standardized tests can accurately assess progress or placement on any given curriculum. For maximum validity, teachers should have curriculum-based tests–tests that sample skill presented on the curriculum in actual use. Mastery and progress toward mastery of curricular objective is what needs to be measured. Tests that are specific to particular curricula are necessary to do this.

Predictive validity is the extent to which a test predicts later performance in a skill area of concern. Predictive validity is an important consideration when selecting readiness tests. Readiness tests are necessary to head off failure. Readiness tests need sufficient predictive accuracy to identify children who are at risk for failure. Intervention at the readiness level is far more productive than pushing a student into instructional activities that are too difficult.

High predictive validity is difficult to achieve. After all, a skill not yet attained does not readily provide items for a test. Remember, content validity is achieved by making sure that components of the skill comprise the test. However, on readiness tests, items that seem to be sub skills of the criterion skill are about all that can be used. Readiness tests, especially reading readiness tests, cannot predict all levels of later reading achievement with accuracy. However, they can do one very important job of prediction quite well; readiness tests do identify children who will have trouble in learning to read. Here rests the importance of readiness tests and predictive validity. Readiness tests with sufficient predictive validity to predict likelihood of failure need to be adopted. More important than their adoption and use, the information obtained from them needs to be acted upon.

Reliability is a characteristic of valid tests. Reliable tests are dependable; they five consistent results. Reliable test are made up of well constructed, unambiguous items. Reliability and validity are occasionally confused because the coefficients used for both are the same (from 0.00 to 1.00); there is a necessary relationship between the two. Reliability is a necessary characteristic of a valid test, but a test that gives consistent results does not necessarily measure the thing you want it to. Reliability is primarily important because it is necessary for validity.

Reliability becomes an important consideration for teachers constructing informal or curriculum-referenced tests for classroom use. These are the most-used tests in teaching. In the formulation of tests, unless care is taken to reduce error caused be ambiguous or confusing test items, inaccurate assessment information will result.

Types of Tests

Norm-referenced tests constitute a considerable portion of published tests. Norm-referenced means that they have been given to groups representing certain populations. These may be populations assembled by age, sex, grade level, geographic area, etc. With these tests, depending on the normative information furnished, the performance of an individual can be compared with the norms, or a group's performance can be compared with the normative group performance.

I have been stressing the use of curriculum-based tests. However, norm-referenced tests may be used in a variety of beneficial ways. Reading readiness tests may be used in a variety of beneficial ways. Reading readiness tests are typically norm-referenced. Norm-referenced tests can be used in program evaluation or for accountability. However, they usually are not helpful in determining specific instructional objectives, unless the items on the test correspond very closely to those that make up the curriculum. Usually these tests can sample only a few items from any level of a curriculum and so can provide only limited guidance for instruction.

Criterion-referenced tests were developed to provide more guidance for instruction. Criterion-referenced tests differed from norm-referenced tests in that they sere designed to evaluate an individual's level of performance or mastery of some specific instructional objectives. Actually curriculum-based assessment does this. The word "curriculum" was specifically selected to indicate that the instructional objectives to be measured must be those taken from the curriculum that is guiding instruction. Also, many so-called criterion-referenced tests are published for general use and are unlikely to represent a specific curriculum criterion. Some criterion-referenced tests have been based on well defined scope and sequence of skills in curricular areas such as arithmetic. In these cases the tests can make estimable curricula in their own right and so have been adopted as curricula and thereby become curriculum-based tests as well.

In recent years, I have seen the development of criterion-referenced tests with norms and norm-referenced tests that have criterion-referenced interpretations. Consequently the distinction between the two has diminished somewhat.

Screening tests should be used to avoid placing children in failure situations. Also, they should be used to discover which children are making less progress in reading than they might potentially achieve. Vision, hearing and readiness tests should be routinely administered for these reasons. These tests may be used to refer children for further evaluation. Screening tests may lack precision. However, inaccuracy in the direction of over-referral from such tests is preferable to under-referral.

Low-stakes screening tests, particularly reading tests, should be given annually. Every teacher, in every grade and every subject should be apprised of the current reading skill level of each of their students. Too few teachers are aware of the instructional reading level of their students. They are often astonished to learn that the reading skill level of a quarter of the students in their classrooms is insufficient to cope with reading difficulty of the texts and instructional material assigned that grade or subject. Non- intrusive, informal reading tests show this essential readiness level for instruction at all grades and most subjects.

Diagnostic tests refer to assessment procedures that are used to identify the specific needs of students with learning problems. They are often associated with the identification of the cause of the problem, the classification of the handicapping condition or the labeling of children. Some notions of diagnostic assessment make it a guide to instructional procedure. This has been called diagnostic-prescriptive teaching or simply prescriptive teaching. In this approach to teaching, assessment is carefully articulated with the instruction provided. This is precisely the intent of curriculum-based assessment. However, so-called diagnostic tests seldom accurately sample skill deficiency specific to any one particular curriculum. In fact, if one chooses to use some diagnostic test then one is obliged to teach to the revealed deficiencies as though the test were the curriculum. This phenomenon causes a set of difficulties that frequently confound the problem of the instruction of low-achieving and learning disabled students— but more will be said about this later.

Proponents of diagnostic tests 2nd of prescriptive teaching claim that strengths and weaknesses are assessed. However, the focus of diagnosis and the subsequent intervention typically emphasize weakness or skill deficiency. There are no stated formulas or systematic approaches to balancing the measurement of weaknesses and strength then programming them equally through prescritption.

The term "diagnosis," whether in medicine or education, implies the identification of a problem. However, it is critically important to identify what a child knows or what skills he or she has. Knowledge of strength is necessary to prepare instructional materials and activities that produce success and time engaged in learning. From hard experience, I have found what happens when one falls into the diagnostic trap of identifying deficiencies. A variety of activities are planned to remediate these deficiencies; then it is found that these activities are frustrating and nonproductive for the student. These unfortunate situations occur because the work is made up entirely of activities that the students don't know and can't do well or at all. They are the deficiencies reveal through diagnosis. The students are systematically, if unwittingly, overwhelmed with work that is too difficult.

With the form of CBA advocated here. Diagnostic information focuses on strength more than weakness. Success is produced by appropriately balancing knowns with unknowns in all instructional activities. Strengths must overwhelmingly predominate. I will say much more about this feature of CBA later.

Case histories can provide insight into students' learning problems through knowledge of their background and development.

Some information will have immediate relevance to the remedial action taken in the classroom. How much children have had to eat or how much sleep they get will affect their behavior at school. What languages are spoken will influence curricular needs. Children's health, both physical and emotional, will affect their school performance.

Information concerning the past and present status of a child in family and community is important. Health and nutritional information are equally important. Children with empty stomachs are more likely to benefit from a sandwich than from a curricular adjustment.

Avoiding Failure

The time to prevent failure in school is before instruction starts. We are in a rush to start instruction and when it is begun, we make every effort to force children to achieve at grade level or to arbitrarily set standards. Hatch (2002) forcefully illustrates how curricular standards are being pushed down into early childhood programs to the detriment of children as young as 3 and 4. Holding all children to the same standard guarantees that some will face failure.

Readiness assessment is important. It is more important that information that suggests the lack of readiness be acted on. If children are not ready to deal with curricular demands and standards placed in the preschool, kindergarten, or first grade; there are several options that should be available on their behalf. These options include a delay of starting first grade, compensatory readiness programming or an extension of the readiness period from a few months to even a year or two.

Readiness test have been criticized for being imprecise measures. For example, the predictive validity of popular reading-readiness tests ranges from about .50 to.70. These coefficients are obtained by correlating these tests scores with level of reading achievement at the end of the first grade. Such coefficients do not permit accurate prediction of the level of reading achievement for individual students. However, these tests do perform remarkably well in predicting which children will fail. The most important use of readiness tests is to locate kindergarten age children who are likely to fail and not to predict specific achievement levels.

Standardized reading-readiness tests accurately identify about 80 percent of the children who are not ready.

However, when using such tests, the results should be moderated by teacher judgment. Obviously, some children will fail who are not identified by readiness tests. They will fail because of factors not sampled by the tests. For these children, teacher judgement and the information gained from case histories will be the only means of identifying potential failure.

Assessment for Teaching

Curriculum-referenced tests should be used to identify a child's current level of functioning within the curriculum in use. A starting place or a readiness level is most accurately established with curriculum-referenced tests. Curriculum-referenced tests are made up of curriculum items. Only with this degree of specificity can validity be insured. The level a child can reasonably be expected to achieve on a particular curriculum can only be found by determining the child's readiness level which is his or her current level of mastery. This is the point from which instruction can comfortably proceed. It is a comfortable instructional level, and it can be determined with a test that adequately samples items from the scope and sequence of skills that make up the curriculum. Some reading and math programs provide progress or placement tests that can be used to measure some of their components, but accurate placement is determined by the evaluation of the student's performance on various levels of activities or reading selections sampled from those that will be a part of daily instruction. The levels being sought are called the basal and instructional levels. These levels were first defined by Emmett Betts (1946) in regard to reading difficulty levels. The nature and details of basal and instructional levels will be covered in the next chapter, but briefly, for reading, the basal level (also known as the independent level) is the highest reading difficulty level where a student encounters no more unknown words than one in fifty and has a comprehension level of at least 90 percent. The instructional level ranges from the basal level to the point at which the student encounters a maximum of one new word in twenty-five and has a comprehension level of at least 75 percent. The instructional level marks the maximum difficulty level where a student can remain on task without symptoms of tension and frustration.

Besides the assessment to determine readiness, entry level or instructional level, there must be direct evaluation with and of the instructional activities and materials in daily use. In CBA, evaluation is a central component of instruction itself. It is fundamentally checking the instructional match between activity or material and the student it is being used with. This is not as great a chore as it may sound. Already, seat work, worksheets, and homework are routinely checked. We routinely listen to children reading orally. We usually use this information to give grades on daily work. Essentially the same procedure is followed with the routine of curriculum-based assessment, but instead of assigning a grade to the student, the information is used to see if an instructional level match has been made. For example, if the student has missed too many items on the math worksheet that will suggest that there are too many new or hard items for him to manage. The material might require further examination to see if the student has the prerequisite skills necessary to do the items that were missed. When listening to a child's oral reading, the number of words he stumbles over or can't identify should not suggest a letter grade but the appropriateness for that child. In effect, we should grade the material or activity not the child.

If the child does not or cannot complete assigned work, the difficulty level of the work should be reviewed. If a child is frequently off task or shows signs of tension and frustration when he is, the difficulty level of the work should be studied. The very processes of instruction are assessment information when it is curriculum based.

Acting on information gained in this way means that the curriculum level must be gauged individually. An individual's maximum progress will only occur if he is given work that he or she can stay on-task with and complete with comprehension. These are simply the conditions that exist for virtually all students who are making adequate or better progress in school, and we should expect no less for our slow and disabled learners. These are conditions that produce success and progress. In order to achieve these conditions for students who have low achievement and learning disabilities, assessment must be an intimate part of daily instruction. All instruction should be viewed as a form of assessment. But remember; this will be more assessment of instruction and material than of student. It is necessary to observe and record the student's performance, but the grade is reserved for the instructional activity itself.

Test Relevance

Choose your tests well for they will likely become your curriculum. Witness the coming of the standards movement and the high-stakes tests that accompany the standards. Teachers nationwide devote increasing time teaching to these tests. It is important for their students to pass the tests, and it is important for their teachers who will be held accountable for theirs students' performance. I have no argument whatever with teaching to a test; that is essentially what curriculum-based assessment is about. If the objectives measured on the tests are important, then they should be taught. These high-stakes tests are then dictating the contents of the curriculum. I would hope that the curriculum in use is compatible with the contents of the tests. If they are not compatible, then the curriculum should be abandoned for one that is, or the high-stakes tests should simply be adopted as a part of the curriculum. We can only hope that the high-stakes being developed and adopted have content worth teaching to.

"Teaching the test" should not be a pejorative expression. You should be testing what you teach and teaching what you test. Remember the discussion of "content validity." A test must be comprised of a sufficient number of items from the topic under consideration in order to have content validity. Content validity is attained by using the curriculum as the basis for assessment. Another way of attaining it is to make the test the basis of the curriculum. This will be well and good if the test contains the range of appropriate and desirable items that should be in a curriculum that covers the wide developmental needs of students being administered it.

Often teachers or psychologists administer various tests to children with learning difficulties. A wide variety of such tests are routinely given. The tests themselves may have no relevance to the child's curriculum. However, deficiencies in skills, perception or assorted aptitudes are invariably found. Often the deficiency has nothing to do with what is going on in instruction. Yet, the identification of the deficiency prompts the development of an ancillary remedial curriculum to deal with this supposed deficit. Sometimes these new curricula replace or parallel the existing program. Often this new intervention, which was based on noncurriculum-referenced tests, only fragments or dilutes the time spent on regular curricular activities. Children who need more time actively engaged in reading or math activities on their regular curriculum are getting less. These new tests have dictated new curricula. Remember, choose your tests well for they may become your curriculum.

Some standardized reading diagnostic tests are intended to measure word-identification sub skills. Tests of such subskills are unlikely to have content validity when they are compared with specific reading curricula. A wide variety of reading subskills forms a large of virtually all reading programs. These word-identification (decoding or phonics) subskills are presented in different emphasis and sequences from one to the next. Take the division of opinion about whether consonant or vowel rules are most important to teach. Reutzel and Cooter (2004) in their book, *Teaching Children to Read,* say, "Arguably the single most efficient phonics generalization to teach is *beginning consonant sounds in words*" (p. 111). But, Carnine, Silbert, Kame'enui, and Tarver (2004) in their book, *Direct Instruction Reading* (4th Ed.), say, "Vowels are the most useful letters" (p. 61). Skills considered important in one reading program may be overlooked in the next. Published tests cannot sample the scope and sequence of subskills presented in a given reading curriculum unless they are prepared for that curriculum. When noncurriculum-based tests are administered to children with reading problems, they will very likely show sub skill deficiencies measured by those tests. However, they may not be the ones that have been or are being presented in the curriculum to those children. The danger with using such tests is that the evidence of deficiency may produce a program to remediate it. A new curriculum based on invalid evidence may be started. The new curriculum displaces time that might be used with the regular curriculum. Achievement is not enhanced.

Reading curricula are often designed to fit test results. This is a basic tenet of prescriptive teaching. A subskill deficiency on some diagnostic test does not necessarily mean that more and more emphasis should be placed on teaching that subskill. Do not let supposed subskills dominate either assessment or the reading curriculum. The author has witnessed situations where students receive whole remedial programs based on subskill deficits, few of which are common to the regular curriculum. Teachers vest tremendous credibility in published tests. A poor reader did poorly on these tests; therefore, deficiencies revealed by them must be remediated. The cause of the reading problem is the deficits revealed by these tests. Validity is almost never considered. The students who are the recipients of this practice are not beneficiaries. The bulk of reading instruction centers on learning subskills that have been carefully identified as missing; adequate success is not considered, and worst of all; time that could have been spent at really reading is virtually eliminated.

Measures of actual reading from the reading material that is available in the curriculum are the most important gauge of reading progress and the best guides to formulating specific instructional activities. Two types of informal assessment are most useful. One is word-recognition assessment (the difference between word-recognition and word-identification will be considered in a later chapter). These tests should be based on the words being introduced in a student's reading program and words that have the highest frequency and utility. The other is the assessment of silent and oral reading of specific selections from the student's reading material. These two types of tests should be used to determine the placement, to check achievement after teaching and to evaluate and prepare reading materials for specific children.

Teaching and Testing

The use of instructional material that is too difficult results in failure and with failure goes its attendant behaviors. On the other hand, these same behaviors can be the cause rather than the result of failure. In this case, the focus of instruction must include an emphasis on the control of the interfering behavior. If the difficulty of the material is the cause of a student's off-task behavior, then it is a matter of adjusting the instructional materials. However, this will also be necessary even if the behaviors themselves are contributing to the learning problems. One cannot simply focus on behavior without attending to the difficulty of the activity being taught.

The first stage of assessment is to find out how much ability the student has and then prepare or identify the activity or material that will fit within that skill level. This material should maintain attention and be completed with comprehension. This is the instructional level. The instructional level will be a subject of the next chapter.

After the instructional level has been identified, the second stage of assessment can occur. This is observation of students working at an appropriate level of difficulty. The off-task behaviors that remain after sufficient opportunity to get used to working at this level are then the focus of assessment. The persisting off-task behaviors may well be the cause of a learning problem and can require an intervention that gives specific attention to modifying them. In other words, when a child remains inattentive or distracted from instructional activities that are clearly within his or her ability, the attention problem, the distractibility or any other off-task behaviors will need dealing with. However, ample time must be provided to observe the child working at carefully prepared instructional level activities. Children who have experienced nothing but failure and frustration in school, often for years, will have developed a set attitude and behavior pattern when facing any instructional activity. However, finding success in an activity that usually produces discomfort is so immediately rewarding that most students are very shortly on task.

The best form of intervention is most accurately determined by the observation of residual behaviors as was outlined above. It is only in this way that a teacher can be certain of whether off-task behavior is a cause or a symptom and which must be dealt with.

Much of the data for identifying or preparing instructional material must come from the continued observation and testing that occurs during teaching. The preparation of instructional material will be necessary as long as the student's instructional level and need for repetition and practice lie outside that provided by the available published material. For example, through teaching and testing a teacher will determine the amount of repetition of a word a child needs to learn it. In basal reading programs, and in literature based programs, there is inconsistent, often spotty repetition of words once they have been introduced. This is a major problem for the low achieving student. The teacher will of necessity provide the required additional repetition for these words in supplementary activities if the student is to get any benefit from the basal reader at all.

Finding Problems

Unfortunately, it most often takes a student's failure to confirm the existence of a problem. Failure should not be our primary identification instrument. Children should never be required to fail before appropriate instructional steps are taken. Failure occurs in two ways, one obvious the other not. Failure is obvious when a child falls behind the ongoing level of instruction. This inability to work at grade level stands out, and it is frequently accompanied by other distracting behaviors. The less obvious failure occurs when a student has a potential for achievement that is higher than his grade level of placement but is functioning well only at that placement level. There will be no failure related behavior because the instructional demands do not exceed the child's ability. For this reason, the problem is quite likely to go unnoticed. Some would not call this failure, but it certainly is failure to achieve to potential.

Among those who cannot perform at grade-level standards, there is a common cause. That cause is their failing work. Failure is not productive, so the more a child fails the further he or she falls behind her or his potential.

A problem exists if a student is not achieving to the level that the student's capacity or potential indicates. Therefore, a measure of potential is required to determine the existence of such a problem or discrepancy.

At the elementary levels relevant measures of reading potential are listening comprehension tests. If selections are taken from each of the grade levels of reading materials being used by the students, then the test will be curriculum-based.

The procedure for preparing a listening comprehension test is the same as for preparing an informal reading inventory. However, instead of the student reading the test to find his instructional reading level, the teacher reads the test aloud to the student to find the highest level where the student attains at least 70 percent comprehension. This is the student's listening comprehension level. It indicates the level of reasonable reading achievement potential for the student. You can learn to read language that is unfamiliar only in print.

This informal approach to determining reading capacity level is curriculum-based. It is directly related to the reading materials that are to be used. Thus, the relevance and validity of the measurement is insured.

Many commercially prepared reading inventories may be used as reading capacity tests. That is if they made up of well graded passages, passages that are matched with considerable precision to the readability level of each grade. The reliability of the comprehension questions should have been established. If there is a discrepancy, it can be determined by using the inventory to measure both the instructional reading level and the listening capacity level. This is done in the same way as with the teacher-made, curriculum-based test that was described above. However, the commercially prepared tests may lack the relevance and precision that the curriculum-based tests have.

Intelligence tests are used to determine capacity or potential. Intelligence tests have fairly high correlations with academic achievement. They are typically required in the identification of learning disabled children. Here, a discrepancy between achievement and the potential established by the score on an "intelligence" test is used to verify the existence of a learning disability. This degree of precision may be sufficient for administrative purposes, but for the teacher, the more relevant curriculum-based procedures are useful for instruction.

Changes in Assessment

Assessment that serves the instructional needs of students is curriculum-based. Fitting the curriculum to a student to produce success and reasonable, attainable levels of achievement requires new directions and new objectives for assessment. These differences have been the subject of this chapter. No new techniques or tests have been revealed. The techniques and tests are standard, even mundane. How they relate to instruction, however, is quite different than standard practice.

One difference is the notion of curriculum-basing; this seems to legitimize "teaching to the test." From the inception of CBA, it has been called the ultimate in teaching to the test (Tucker, 1985). This is all true but in the best sense. Curriculum basing insures test validity and the relevance of the instruction that results from such measurement.

Another difference is that assessment's main function is to insure success in instructional activities. Therefore, assessment information is used to prepare appropriate instructional level activities and materials for each student.

Insuring success requires a different focus of assessment. If success is the focus of assessment, the data of evaluation is used to grade the materials or the activities appropriateness of fit to the student. The instructional activity or material is graded more so than the student. Further, attending to success means that instruction must be used as assessment. The normal grading or scoring of seatwork, homework, drill, etc. takes on an institutionalized status. It is the regular ongoing fundamental form of the bulk of curriculum-based assessment. However, it is not for the purpose of giving the students a grade; it is to make certain there is an instructional match between curriculum level and student.

Another difference is the shift in focus from weaknesses to strengths of a student. Children who have made painfully small amounts of progress have few, often well concealed strengths. Primary attention must be given to finding them. Success must be built on strengths and skills. In instructional level reading known words out number unknowns at least ninety-six to four. Attention maintaining drill and seatwork in math require that only about a quarter of the items can be made up of still fewer (3 to 5) new and unfamiliar ones. The rest of the items must be more familiar one that are being reviewed and practiced for fluency or automaticity. In all instances the ratio side of known and familiar dominate. Known words are the helpful context in reading that support the identification of the new and unknown words. They may provide helpful contextual support in math drill work. Finally, the high proportion of knowns permits students to feel the reinforcement of success and accomplishment that is routine for their higher achieving peers.

Another difference is the observation of off-task behavior. Off-task behavior results from a poor instructional match. However, if there is persisting off-task behavior after a good match is made, then an additional curricular emphasis dealing with the behaviors may be appropriate.

Standardized testing is not emphasized in CBA, but it is used. It has two primary functions. One is in preventing failure. The use of readiness tests is an important function here. Accountability and program evaluation is another appropriate use. Norm-referenced measures here can provide information on how well the teacher or program is performing given similar students and circumstances.

A novel difference exists between curriculum based assessment and most other forms of assessment. If norm-referenced tests are given to the students in any classroom, a great variation in scores on the tests would be expected. We expect this wide variation scores on any test administered to the group whether teacher-made or standardized. However, with curriculum-based assessment, one is trying to achieve approximately the same scores from all the students. The curriculum itself is used to form the test, and if the level of the curriculum is adjusted appropriately to fit the individual students instructional needs, then the scores should reflect that these needs have been met. In other words, curricular materials vary in difficulty; scores stay about the same level which indicates that the students are meeting with success. This is a major change from standard practice where test scores must vary because curriculum materials and activities are kept at a relatively uniform level. CBA is a tuning process where level of instruction is continually matched with student skill. Instructional delivery is tuned to the student by making sure that performance in the instructional material stays within the prescribed limits. Really, the tests themselves vary because they are comprised of the actual instructional material being used with individual students.

Instruction and assessment are fused in this system. How assessment is integrated in instructional activities and how assessment is used to prepare instructional activities and materials are the subjects of subsequent chapters.

Chapter 4

INSTRUCTIONAL LEVELS AND
RATES IN READING

The match between a student and the curriculum needs to be made very specifically. This match must be made at the specific level of instructional activity in material that is used to achieve curricular goals. It is at this daily level of activity where the student must meet with instruction that produces the success, comprehension, on-task behavior and learning time that is needed to achieve. The subject of this chapter is the nature of instructional activity and material that must be provided in this match. CBA is the matching process; instructional levels and rates are the criterion indexes of the accuracy of the match.

Assessment is used to make the match initially, and it is used throughout instruction to maintain it. Instructional activities and materials do not have some built in or fixed level of difficulty. The level of difficulty is relative to individual students. For example, the designation of a grade level of difficulty for some basal reading material is at best only a normative index. In other words, the material is appropriate for the "average" student in this age range. Actually, however, the only way that the difficulty level of any instructional material can be determined for a specific child is by letting that child use it to see how hard it actually is. Fundamentally, this is what curriculum based assessment does, and it is done as a part of all instructional activity.

The instructional level of any material exists only in regard to the individuals who use it. It can be said that there is a normative level and an instructional level for instructional material. A normative level is the level usually stated by the publisher of the material. It can be determined by a readability formula or by testing it with groups of children. Sometimes even more subjective methods such as "leveling" (Fry, 2002) are used to determine difficulty level, but whatever the method, at best, it can only approximate the difficulty level for groups of students, not individuals. The instructional level is determined by measuring a student's performance in that particular material.

The nature of a student's performance on some specific material determines its instructional level for that student. The nature of this performance can be quantified, and this quantified performance can be compared to objective performance standards that indicate the instructional level. If there is a gap between the student's performance and the standards then different materials need to be obtained or the materials need to be modified so that the match can be made.

Teaching as Testing

Teachers must view what they are teaching as a test. The student's performance is the test's results. There are important results to be noted on the student's performance in each teaching activity: The number of words a student does not know and her or his fluency when reading orally; his response to questions that indicate the comprehension level of a selection just read; the percent correct on a word-identification worksheet or a drill activity in math. This is just to mention a few of the activities that produce measurable responses; virtually all of teaching does just this. These responses form the basis for judgments about the difficulty level of a specific material or activity for a specific student. Making the match between student and instruction only requires a little more systematic observation of performance during daily activities.

Usually when performance on daily activity is noted, it is for the purpose of assigning grades. However, it should be for the purpose of identifying, adjusting or maintaining the appropriate difficulty level of instruction for the students. Poor performance is indicative of a poor match between student and instructional material. When students are constantly performing poorly in school, primary test evidence is being ignored.

Observation of performance on daily activities can provide the essential information on how to make an accurate match between student and instructional level and instructional rate. The subject of this chapter is the characteristics of instructional level activities and materials.

Instructional Level in Reading

Gates (1930) first addressed the problem of vocabulary burden in beginning reading instruction. When Gates began studying the problem of vocabulary burden in the 1920s, the available primary reading material introduced new words in the range of 1 in 10 to 1 in 17 running words. These introduction rates had proven far too difficult, and teachers routinely had to provide much supplementary teacher-made material to enable their students to read these books at all. Though he found that an introduction rate of one new word in 150 was necessary for the slower readers, it was to slow for the more able ones. He found that one new word in 60 was a manageable rate for a majority of beginning readers. Beginning in the 1930s, basal readers generally conformed to his guidelines for word introduction. His research made beginning reading materials accessible to a majority of students.

Controlling the introduction of words in reading instructional materials was an important step, but simply controlling the introduction of words does not mean that the new vocabulary load is the same or will remain the same for all students. A word may remain unfamiliar even as many new ones are being introduced. Emmett Betts (1946) studied the problem of how many strange printed words students can manage in a reading activity before their comprehension breaks down, and they show signs of frustration. This difficulty level was the "ceiling" of difficulty. He called this level the "frustration level" and it was to be avoided. The difficulty level appropriate for instruction he called the "instructional level." The instructional level had a vocabulary burden between the "basal" or "independent" level and the frustration level. Betts identified the basal/independent level as the highest reading level at which a student encountered almost no unknown words and had complete comprehension. The students could read such materials independently entirely on their own and it was appropriate for recreational reading.

In general, the instructional level of reading difficulty occurs when a student encounters new or unknown words in the range of 2 to 4 percent. With a vocabulary load of this size, students can usually attain a comprehension level of about 75 percent, if they are receiving some teaching assistance. At the basal/independent level students should encounter fewer than 2 percent unknown words and have a comprehension level of at least 90 percent.

At the independent level, students can gain fluency and expand their instant word recognition mastery. They gain confidence in reading. It is the level that indicates their level of reading mastery. Here they can learn to enjoy reading as a recreational activity. It is very important for all students to have access to independent level reading materials. As Allington (2002) pointed out, we do not sufficiently appreciate the importance of having lots of easy reading material for all students.

The instructional level is important because it gives the maximum leeway for introducing new words, while permitting comprehension and attention maintenance.

There are sufficient numbers of known words to supply supportive context to aid in the identification of the new and unfamiliar words. It is the level at which the application of word identification skills can be fruitfully practiced and improved. Word recognition vocabulary can grow optimally.

The frustration level is nonproductive and is to be avoided. When a student encounters more than about four percent new words (about one new word in 25), signs of stress appear and comprehension breaks down rapidly. Children given frustration level work will demonstrate little on-task behavior in silent reading, and their oral reading will show clear evidence of the number of words unknown to them.

In order to remind the mature reader of what it is like to cope with the number of unknown words that beginning readers encounter, several selections have been prepared. These selections use obscure or contrived words to insure that the same impact is made. The first selection has about 7 percent unknown words:

The man leaned against the current as he waded, waist-deep, upstream. His hands steadied either end of the furnwunch balanced across his shoulders. He had moved about 90 yards from the denup where he had entered the stream. A few yards ahead, a part of the wooded bank had been replaced by an acnrid frud. He came abreast of it, and with effort, pressed the furnwunch up and over his head, and then set it on top of the frud. He placed his hands on his hips, pulled his elbows back and arched his back in an attempt to stretch out muscles that were knotted from the prolonged exertion.

He relaxed somewhat and began a visual inspection of the frud. He moved closer to it and reached under the water to explore its surface. Moving slowly, he started the search from the downstream end. At about the rondtip he stopped and probed one area intently. Satisfied that he had located a grundle he continued to the upstream end. There was only one grundle to contend with. He retrieved the furnwunch and cradled the heavy implement as he made his way back to the rondtip. He gingerly lowered the furnwunch, holding it perpendicular to the frud. When it reached the grundle, he slid it in its full length. He held it in place with one hand and turned the expansion lock handle until the instrument was seated tightly in place. His mission accomplished, he was clearly relieved. He waded easily downstream to the dnup.

The passage is about 250 words in length. It contains only six unknown words. However, the words are repeated so that there are a total of sixteen occurrences. This amounts to about seven percent unknown words in the passage. The passage would have seemed far more difficult if all of these occurrences had been of different words. Each time a new word is repeated in a context of known words, it attracts additional semantic substance. This passage, however, had too many unknowns to provide the kind of supportive context that is needed to figure out what an unknown word is or means. Consequently, comprehension of the passage will be extremely limited.

If the number of different unknown words is limited, a passage like the one above can be within the instructional level. This will be true only if there is a provision for introducing the unknown words before the passage is read, or providing some means for identifying them during the reading activity. If each new word in the passage is counted only once, then the number of unknowns amounts to less than three percent, which is within the instructional range.

The following selection is at the frustration level in any case:

> Long radians were forming when Matthew arrived. He tried to phindate the amount of time it would take to get to the convorster. Vort it would be too long, plast he would miss the game. He vraxated for a moment until the radians became even longer. He decided that he would ordrul in the radian opet see vort it would start moving more expeditiously. No sooner had he started fleedjuul, when it began opet mostulalag quite hard. Matthew became disgusted, sipped up his ornaforger, and walked back to his car. He drove home ov the mostul. By the time he put the car in the garage, the mostul was droim, and the faedos was out. Matthew was doubly disgusted now. Sullenly, he went inside to watch the game. He turned on the television set but nothing happened. Matthew said to himself, "What a lousy frol!"

In this passage, thirteen new words are introduced or about nine percent of the total words. The percentage may sound small but the effect on intelligibility is large.

If a student is required to read a passage of similar difficulty orally, the symptoms of frustration level reading would be readily apparent. The refusals to pronounce and the mispronunciations of the unknown words would be the most obvious symptom. The reading would be halting at best, with many slowdowns and stoppages at the new words. Answers to questions directed to the student about the content and meaning of the story would be, at best, guessed at. This is pretty much the behavior the reader would demonstrate if required to read the above passage and then someone privy to the meaning of all the words in the passage asked the comprehension questions.

The next passage is prepared at a level approaching the independent/basal reading level. Less than two percent of the words are unknown.

> Nathan heard the rubbing sound again. He pulled himself further into the sleeping bag and closed it over his head. There was the sound again! This time the whole tent shook a little. Nathan wished that he had the flashlight with him in the sleeping bag. He was sure an orgillon was trying to get in the tent. Jeff had said that an orgillon would go away if you shined a light on it. Nathan tried to be completely quiet, hoping that the orgillon would think no one was in the tent. It didn't work. The rubbing and shaking became louder. With all the courage Nathan could muster, he slipped an arm out of the sleeping bag and felt around for the flashlight. He found it and not a pezot too soon. He felt something standing on the sleeping bag. He switched the light on and there, to his surprise and relief, was Gruffy, the pet goat.

The abundance of familiar context helps dealing with the unknown words in this passage. The appearance of unknown words is disconcerting, but the context here has sufficient strength to supply much of the necessary meaning to maintain a high level of comprehension.

An important difference exists between the levels of difficulty illustrated above and difficulty levels children encounter. This difference is that the unknown words in the children's material should be unfamiliar only in print. This is also a fundamentally important readiness requirement for beginning reading; all of the words should be familiar if spoken or read to the children. In other words, the spoken counterpart of the words is familiar. In this case, familiar context with other word-identification skills should assist the students in calling to mind the familiar spoken counterpart of words that are unfamiliar only in print. So, rather than only speculating on the meaning of the unknown words, the student should be able to identify the unknown words without undue effort. Without the support of much known context, the effort required to identify the unknown words is too great and is frustrating. With so much attention necessary in the identification of unknown words, the thread of comprehension will be lost or ignored.

An important attribute of the instructional and independent reading levels, is that they permit and foster time engaged in reading. Research on academically engaged time or academic learning time, shows the direct relationship between the amount of time spent on reading achievement (Allington, 2002; Gickling & Thompson, 1985; Rosenshine & Berliner, 1978).

Much has been said about interest and motivation concerning reading materials. However, there is no substitute for supplying students with appropriate instructional level materials. Frustration level materials are neither interesting nor motivating.

Repetition Rates in Reading

How long does it take to learn a word? Far too little attention has been given to this question. Yet, we know that low-achieving and learning disabled students are deficient in the number of "sight words" they know or in the size of their "word recognition" vocabulary. They just don't know enough words to use their basal readers. Gates (1930) did the primary work in answering this question many years ago. This important, but neglected, work suggests the basic guidelines for providing repetition. He studied the repetition requirements of children by levels of intelligence. Table 1 shows Gates's suggested guidelines for word repetition in connected discourse. His findings have been reviewed and reconfirmed (Hargis, Terhaar-Yonkers, Williams, & Reed, 1988).

Table 1
MEAN NUMBER OF WORD REPETITIONS REQUIRED
BY IQ LEVELS

Repetitions	IQ
20	120-129
30	110-119
35	90-109
40	80-89
45	70-79
55	60-69

Adapted from Gates (1930).

Gates emphasized that these numbers were averages and that there was considerable individual variation in the repetition requirements for various words.

Some words are more difficult to learn than others. The characteristic that dominates the learnability of words is imagery level. Imagery level or concreteness of words has to do with how easily a mental image is formed of the referent each word represents. Concrete nouns will have the highest imagery level. They are words like cat, dog, chair, tree, car, bird, etc. Low imagery nouns are words like idea, time, mile, error, belief, etc. High imagery facilitates learning to recognize new words.

Other parts of speech have imagery levels as well. Verbs, adjectives and adverbs can have various levels of imagery; however, the mental image is not distinct from the things they modify or operate with. To be concrete, the verb *run*, requires a concrete, animate noun as its subject. Consider this sentence: *The rabbit ran through the grass.* But with an abstract subject it will not be concrete. Consider the sentence: *Several ideas ran through her mind.* Adjectives also require a noun, and adverbs may require an entire sentence. Imagery level remains, however, an important factor in their ease of learning.

Other quite common words, sometimes called function words, have very low imagery levels. These words are articles, auxiliary verbs, relative pronouns, subordinating conjunctions, coordinating conjunctions, etc. It is simply not possible to form a mental image of words like *been, are, that, which at, some, of,* etc. Teachers through the ages have noted the difficulty that some of these most common words have caused beginning readers.

Several research projects have been conducted to determine the differences in difficult of learning to recognize these various kinds of words by their imagery level (Hargis & Gickling, 1978; Gickling, Hargis & Radford, 1981; Hargis, 1978). Findings here point out that high imagery significantly enhances the development of word recognition, if the words are presented in isolation (the words were presented on flash cards).

Subsequent research has demonstrated the facilitating effect of context on the lower imagery words (Hargis, Terhaar-Yonkers, Williams, & Reed, 1988). In this research, the words were placed in sentences within stories based on experiences. Each of the experimental words was placed in the context of sentences made up of familiar words. This kind of context had a greatly facilitating effect on lower imagery words. Meaningful, familiar context makes low imagery words as learnable as high imagery words. The study was conducted with a group of low-achieving and learning disabled students. The low imagery words required an average of 58 repetitions in isolation and 47 repetitions in context. There was no significant difference for high imagery nouns. They required about the same repetitions in context or isolation.

Notice, though, the amount of repetition required to learn to recognize a word. This need for repetition is unremitting. If these children are to learn to read words, the words require a great deal of repetition. It is preferable that the repetition be provided in meaningful contextual settings whenever possible.

The Dolch Basic Sight Word List (1941) is made up of words most associated with word recognition teaching. These words are often called service words or sight words. They are the most common of all English words. These words represent over half the words used in primary level readers (Mangieri, 1977). The majority of the words are function words; there are no high imagery nouns on this list.

The commonness and familiarity of these words belie their difficulty. They are the most difficult words for a beginning reader to learn in isolation. When slow achieving and learning disabled children demonstrate problems in learning to read, extra assistance will often be provided to them in learning these words. Unfortunately, much of the assistance these children receive will be with isolated drill activity, using flash card drills or games. There is an abundance of such material available for these kinds of activities. This approach poses several large problems. A deficit or weakness emphasis is used. The students are drilled on a group of words that are largely unknown, and the opportunity for success is quite reduced. After witnessing more than occasional instances of such practices, seldom was even modest progress in learning the words observed. Children who are less efficient learners are given the least efficient teaching approach.

The meaning or meaningfulness of these words must be provided by their contextual placement in phrases and sentences. The phrase *these dogs* makes the word *these* far more concrete, and each repetition in such an association represents a larger step toward mastery than does its repetition in isolation.

For high imagery words, many meaningful repetitions can occur quite naturally; verbs and other words on traffic signs, names of familiar stores, restaurants, restroom signs, etc. Picture dictionaries utilize the high imagery word with its referent picture combination. However, no one would ever expect to see a sign that said: *where, these, there, as, some, of,* or *are.* Again, children who are having the greatest difficulty learning to read are likely to get less meaningful exposure and repetition.

The need for repetition by these children is not often appreciated. The typical program of instruction in beginning reading does not provide for it.

There is another factor that is also unappreciated: the phonic regularity of words. A word's decodability does not reduce the requirement for repetition to learn it. In other words, the fact that a word is decodable because its letter sound associations are phonically regular, does not lessen the required number of repetitions it needs for mastery.

Imagery level is the most important quality of words when determining need for repetition. This is true primarily for practice given in activities where words are isolated.

At this point, the distinction between **word recognition** and **word identification** should be made. The difference between the two concerns the degree of familiarity of printed words. The term word recognition implies instant recognition of a printed word. Word recognition implies familiarity. Word identification on the other hand is the process of figuring out what a printed word is. This process may be referred to by terms like decoding, phonic analysis, word attack or word identification. Word identification is useful while the process of becoming increasingly familiar with words is underway. Remember; the fact that a student can use word identification skill to figure out a word, in no way reduces that word's need for repetition before it is sufficiently familiar to recognize instantly. It simply means that each repetition can be accomplished with some independence.

Word calling is a behavior associated with a limited word recognition repertoire. A word caller depends on the word identification process to figure out what all of the words are that he or she is reading orally. Word callers read laboriously, word-by-word, "sounding out" or "calling" each word as they try to figure out how to pronounce it. Reading programs that emphasize word identification skills, without providing instructional and independent level reading activities that supply critical repetition, foster word-calling behavior (Hargis, 1982, 1999).

When children begin to demonstrate deficiency in reading achievement, the assumption is often made that they need additional word identification skill training. Consequently, increasing portions of the curriculum for these children is devoted to just that. This training is often separated from instructional level reading activities. So, the very children who require even more meaningful repetition of words will actually get less.

The primary source of reading activity and consequently the primary source of word repetition is the basal reader. The majority of children use basal reading programs when they begin reading. Some fewer learn in children's literature based programs. The amount of repetition they supply is sufficient for most children, if they are also getting some repetition of the same high frequency words in other activities. However, the amount of repetition the basal readers supply is inadequate for lower achieving students (Hargis, 1982, 1985), and it is totally inadequate in the literature-based programs. In both cases, words are not systematically repeated once they are introduced. The repetition that they do receive is quite inconsistent.

There are notable exceptions of works with deficient repetition. All of Dr. Seuss's books beginning with *The Cat in the Hat* are works with tightly controlled vocabularies with excellent repetition. I can only hope for more work with literary merit that provides such nurturing comfort to slow beginning readers.

When words do not get sufficient repetition, increasing numbers of them remain unfamiliar. This increasing load of unknown words makes the material too difficult for instructional purposes. To make a book readable, supplementary teacher-made material must be supplied to provide the necessary repetition of the many words that have remained unfamiliar.

Research on word repetition (Hargis, 1985; Hargis et al., 1988) shows that the decodablity of a word does not affect its requirement for repetition to become familiar. Decodability makes little difference in the learnability of words. That is to say, a phonically irregular word will become part of a student's word-recognition vocabulary as rapidly as a phonically regular one, if the words otherwise share the same imagery characteristics. The place in learning to read, where word identification skill does help with decodable words, is while repetition is still required. Unfamiliar words must be identified over and over again in order to become familiar. Decoding is useful in working independently to get the repetition needed to recognize words instantly.

Decoding is only one method of identifying words. Children will need various kinds of assistance to identify words that are still unfamiliar. The use of context is probably the most universally helpful in identifying words and can complement decoding ability. Also, a tutor, whether teacher, peer, computer or recorder, can supply the word for the students while they still do not recognize it and can't independently identify it. Any of these procedures constitute methods of supplying the necessary repetition. The important thing to remember is that what these children require most, but are least likely to get, is adequate repetition within an instructional level of difficulty.

What they are more likely to get is more work on isolated word identification skills. However, word identification skills can only be efficiently applied if unknown, decodable words appear in the context of reading selections and activities that are at an instructional level of difficulty. Therefore, excessive word identification skill training has limited benefits with low achieving and learning disabled children. Teachers are often heard to say something like, "he knows his phonics, but he still can't read." This should be less surprising than it is. Remember, successful students are applying their word identification skills in instructional level reading activities. The unknown words appear in sufficiently rich contexts and with reasonable frequency. These same conditions are just as necessary for lower achieving students.

Repetition is extremely important in improving the reading ability of learning disabled and low achieving students. The amount of repetition required is not often appreciated. The need for repetition is overlooked because we tend to think that reading deficiency is the result of a subskill deficiency in the student and not the result of a deficiency of repetition of words in the reading material. The assumption may be made that the repetition provided is adequate for most students, so it is adequate for all students. If this is so, then the source of the problem must reside elsewhere. Also, our current diagnostic testing procedures direct our attention away from curricular materials and to the student. However, the deficiency is not in the student; it is in the reading material provided to the student.

The repetition requirements that have just been discussed apply to beginning reading activities. Attention to the need for extra repetition is extremely important for slower students. However, we have good evidence that the need for extremely large amounts of repetition lessens as the student acquire skill and fluency at reading.

Repetition at the Instructional Level

Words are best given repetition at the instructional level. Instructional level reading gives the student an opportunity for real repetition of as yet unfamiliar words. At the instructional level, context is sufficiently rich to assure that identification of the words yet unfamiliar is made. At the frustration levels, context will be less and less helpful as the numberof unknown words increase. Remember; if a word is not identified, its occurrence does not count as a repetition. Real repetition occurs only when a word is identified. It is useless to repeat a word without identification.

There are a variety of ways in which words can be identified for real repetitions. Someone can tell a student what an unknown word is. When a student encounters an unfamiliar word, the teacher, tutor or parent can identify the word for the student. Context alone can be sufficient help in identifying many words. This context can be linguistic or nonlinguistic. Reading selections at the instructional level provide good linguistic context. Words that label things receive this context from the thing that they label. This kind of context is very helpful at beginning reading levels. As students acquire some decoding skill, they can couple the use of context with this emerging skill to identify unfamiliar words independently. Again, the use of decoding skill is most efficiently and effectively applied in reading material which is at the instructional level.

Instructional level reading can be thought of as a guided drill. The material itself provides good supporting context for the identification of words. Decoding skills can be efficiently applied at this level. Children should not be burdened with word identification. When too many words are unfamiliar, reading becomes a painful word-at-a-time reading that fosters the word-calling behavior that was described earlier. Success at word identification is as important as success is in all other aspects of instruction.

Instructional level reading activities should provide the bulk of the repetition requirements for most children. With a manageable burden of unfamiliar words, students can work independently with minimum amounts of guidance. This is very important when working with large groups of students and with a minimum of extra help.

Conclusion

Word introduction and word repetition are the primary considerations in providing reading materials and activities that produce achievement in reading. In their correct measure, they provide instructional level reading activities for individual students. Observation of students while reading provides the basic assessment information as to whether or not the rates match the needs of particular students. The specifics of these assessment techniques will be described in later chapters.

Chapter 5

INSTRUCTIONAL LEVELS AND RATES
IN ARITHMETIC

As with reading instruction, the balance of unknown to familiar constituents determines the instructional level of an arithmetic activity. The ratios are different and the requirements for repetition can be more varied. This will be the subject of this chapter. The levels of difficulty being sought are, however, intended to produce the same effect as in reading. This effect is maximum on-task time, success and achievement. The numbers that will be discussed are the basis for making an instructional match between curriculum and student. Again, the match between a student and the curriculum must be made very specifically. It is made in the daily arithmetic activities that are used to achieve curricular goals. These daily activities are where the student must have instruction to produce success and on-task time. CBA is the matching process; instructional levels and rates are the criterion indexes that show the accuracy of the match.

Assessment that maintains the instructional level match is routine. It is a part of all the assignments and drill activities in which the students engage. It is checking the work, not with giving a grade in mind, but with determining the accuracy of the match between the difficulty of the activity and the skill of the student. Always, the teacher should be striving for the same range of scores. These scores are the numbers which say the instructional match has been made. In classrooms where CBA is used, the scores on assignments will be quite uniform; only the material and activities on which the scores are given will vary. This is quite different from the typical classroom where the scores vary greatly, and the materials and activities are uniform in difficulty level.

The level of a student's performance on a specific assignment determines its instructional level for that student. This level of performance is compared to standards that indicate the instructional level in arithmetic. If there is a gap between the student's performance and this standard, then an adjustment in the difficulty level of the assignment should be made.

Instructional Level in Arithmetic

Appropriate instructional levels in arithmetic are produced by manipulating the introduction rate of new items and then the repetition of the items once they have been introduced. At any given time, the ratio of knowns to unknowns in the instructional activity will determine its appropriateness. New items must be introduced, repeated until they are mastered, and steadily replaced by new items; so that progress along the curriculum is maintained.

The innovator of mathematics teaching, the late Toru Kumon, recognized the critical importance of maintaining the instructional level. In 1954 Toru Kumon was a high school math teacher in Osaka, Japan. His son, about a second-grader, came home with poor marks on his report card in arithmetic. When he critically examined his son's textbook, he designed a home study program for him that required only fine gradations of difficulty from one level to the next. It required his son to get all the practice items correct within a fixed time period before moving on to the next slightly higher level.

By the time his son reached high school he had mastered college level calculus and Mr. Kumon had started an after-school teaching program that was popular across Japan.

How much new information, how many new items, can be introduced at one time? What is an appropriately fine gradation of increased difficulty? In Miller's (1956) classic article, limitations of memory appear to hold this to about seven "pieces" plus or minus two. A more conservative estimate is about five plus or minus two. In introducing new items in arithmetic, the issue is more complex than this relatively simple storage example. The estimates come fairly close, though, when less complex items such as counting and basic facts are presented. This of course can be true only if the student has the readiness skills basic to the presentation of the new items. The important thing to remember is that there are limitations on the amount of new information that can be introduced. Additionally, when planning drill activities, the relative newness of the item may add some memory burden. The fact that an item has been introduced previously and has been subject to some drill does not mean that it cannot contribute difficulty. Certainly, if a student encounters so much unfamiliar material in some drill activity that he can no longer stay on-task or have a reasonable level of success, accuracy, and fluency; it has too many unknown or unfamiliar items on it. Let say three new items make up about 15 to 25 percent of the items on a worksheet for example (Gickling & Thompson, 1985). A range of about 15 to 25 percent new or unfamiliar items in a mixed drill activity will be about as much as a student can handle without frustration and having trouble staying on-task. It should be remembered that these percentages are of things that have been introduced. Students should have some idea of how to deal with them from an initial introduction by the teacher or by its placement in some helpful context. In isolated drill activities, it is likely that all of the drill focuses on the newly introduced items. Here again the activity will be attention maintaining only if the student has had careful introduction to the new items.

In the mixed drill activities about 75 to 85 percent of the items should have been subject to previous drill and should be in various stages of mastery. They are being reviewed for mastery, fluency, accuracy or maintenance. How does the teacher monitor the appropriateness of the introduction rate for individual students? This is done quite simply by checking accuracy of responses which should be considerably higher than the 75 to 85 percent. Certainly they should never be lower.

These scores indicate the appropriate mix of new and review items have been managed. They are fundamental a consideration in managing for success and optimizing achievement. This notion is at times hard for some to accept. It means that all students should be getting essentially the same scores on their work in math most of the time. This is a fundamental change. Instead of using about the same arithmetic material with all the students, thereby producing pronounced variation in scoring; the difficulty level of the material is varied to individual need, thereby producing uniformity in scoring. Remember, this does not mean there is uniformity of achievement. The achievement levels will remain quite varied but higher than under the old system.

With curriculum-based assessment, the scores which are always sought, must be in the same high range for all students. These scores indicate that a match between curriculum and student has been made at the instructional level. Scores should be the same; the materials and activities should vary. This prevents the curriculum from being a Procrustean bed.

Repetition Rates

Practice is an important part of math instruction. How much repetition or practice is required for mastery of a skill? Are there any considerations that affect the amount of repetition? What is mastery itself? What levels of accuracy, i.e., 60, 80, 90 percent, are indicative of mastery? What role does review play in learning?

First of all, repetition—no matter how much—will guarantee learning something if a child is not ready to learn it. Gagne (1970) pointed out that for learning and drill to be effective the program of study must take into account what children know already. One must find out what prerequisites are already mastered and not in a general way but in a precise way for each learner.

When prerequisite skills are carefully presented and learned, use of practice and drill is much optimized and learning much more efficient. Obviously, students are not ready for tasks if they do not have the prerequisite skills. Drill and practice are not nearly as effective in remembering nonsense items as it is in learning concrete meaningful ones. Math items for which prerequisite skills are missing become nonsense items.

Assuming a child has the prerequisite skills for learning a new item, how much drill will then be required? Resnik and Ford (1981) reviewed research related to the relative difficulty of arithmetic problems and the amount of drill they require for mastery. The early research did not attempt to find why problems were easier or harder. It simply ranked them by what seemed to be their ease or difficulty in learning or the number of trials to mastery. The relative difficulty is likely due, however to the amount of mental processing involved in specific problems. Loftus and Suppes (1972) predicted problem difficulty by what they called "structural variables" which seem to contribute to their complexity.

The determinants of the amount of drill required for learning are: readiness (having the prerequisite skills), the complexity of the computational activity and the concreteness of its original presentation. Evidence that the amount of drill is appropriate can be seen in the performance of the individual engaging in it. Is the individual performing at the instructional level? In other words, is the individual practicing learning the correct approach and the correct answers? Poorer performance allows students to learn incorrect approaches and establish error patterns in computation.

Another consideration in regard to drill or practice is "spacing." It is generally known that "spaced" practice is a necessary supplement to "massed" practice for most arithmetic skills. In other words, practice sessions with limited amounts of repetition spaced over several days are more effective than the same amount of practice concentrated in one period.

Isolated drill and mixed drill activities may be considered at different stages of learning. Extended practice involving similar types of problems characterizes isolated drill, while interspersing various types of problems with other types represents mixed drill. It seems that generally the mixed drill is more productive but that isolated drill is best when a new item has first been presented and needs to be established. Also, isolated drill is a helpful remedial procedure in eliminating habituated procedural errors in particular types of computations. Mixed drill is used for maintenance and mastery.

The ultimate function of drill is to increase fluency or rate of response as well as accuracy. The student who is fluent and accurate has reached the level of automatic response to the computational procedure. Ultimately, this will increase the efficiency in problem solving, because the student can handle many of the computational constituents of the problem automatically, thereby reducing the total memory load and time required to determine the answer.

The important thing to remember about a repetition is that it is the association between a new item and the correct answer. Simply providing a certain number of new items in drill activities for a student does not mean that student is getting that many repetitions of the item. Each time a new item occurs, the correct answer to it must be identified. Unless the correct answer is identified, the occurrence does not constitute a repetition leading to mastery. If the student is identifying an incorrect answer the student may be on the road to learning an item incorrectly. This in turn may require a prolonged remedial effort to unlearn the incorrect response and then learn, to mastery, the correct one.

Real repetitions, where the correct answer is linked with the problem, can be made in a variety of ways. A tutor can supply the correct answer each time the student encounters a new or still unfamiliar item. The tutor might be a teacher, a fellow student, a parent, a contextual example, or a computer. The resource of such tutors is not uniformly available, so other provisions need to be made for insuring that a correct response is associated with new items. Massed practice activities which immediately follow a new item's introduction benefit from the short term memory of the student. Real repetition can be provided by placing new items in contexts that are sufficiently strong so as to insure that a correct association is made. Spaced practice then is provided until mastery is achieved.

Eighty percent accuracy on daily activities is adequate for keeping a student on task, but the items missed must still be corrected. The students must have these missed items corrected; the sooner the better. Routine correction of tests and papers is a necessary part of math instruction. The correct repetition must be made. The correction of papers will supply some of the repetition needed for mastery. It doesn't do any good simply to mark items wrong. A good repetition requires making a correct response. The students must see the correct response for all of the items missed before they have the chance to respond incorrectly again.

What level of accuracy is the expected outcome of drill? Ninety percent accuracy is probably sufficient evidence. For basic addition, subtraction, and multiplication facts close to 100 percent is desirable. However, unintentional errors make 90 percent accuracy sufficient for most children in computational activities.

Drill can turn to busy work if it is prolonged with out much increase in accuracy beyond the 90 percent accuracy level. Lesser levels should be accepted in more complex algorithms where several computational procedures compound the likelihood of error.

Concreteness and Meaningfulness

The problem of making arithmetic learning meaningful has been a consideration of educators for many years. On the surface, this important idea may seem rather simple. However two quite different approaches to meaningfulness emerged. Very early the drill and practice of unrelated procedures and facts isolated from application was criticized. Efforts were made to relate each fact and procedure to practical activities where they were needed in dealing with problems of daily living, i.e., making change, measuring a room for carpeting, calculating wages, tips etc. In this way, use and meaning were equated. This seems to have been a rational, practical notion.

At the end of the 1950s, a very different approach to meaningfulness emerged. Now, meaningful learning meant linking underlying structure and concept with the mathematical fact or procedure being learned. This approach is an intellectual one in which meaning is related to knowledge of the structure underlying the fact or process. This is a conceptual approach rather than a computational approach to arithmetic instruction. Resnik and Ford (1981) have a thoughtful review of meaningfulness in mathematics instruction.

Another way that meaningfulness can be viewed quite apart from the two views just discussed has to do with concreteness. This view can be seen in the following example which presents the concept of place-value. A concrete set of objects that can be manipulated might be used to find answers and formulate concepts in regard to place-value. These objects may be any common, convenient-to-manipulate items such as straws, blocks, chips, marbles, etc. The number 76 would be represented by seven sets or stacks of ten chips and one of six; in other words, seven tens plus the six. The students would be directed to the standard notation for the number which this concrete array represents. This concrete procedure is used to assist in teaching an abstract construct which concerns the number system.

The notion of place value, per se, is not necessary in learning a number. It is also very reasonable to learn to regroup ("carry" or "borrow") without being introduced to place-value. Place-value, however, has much to do with understanding the meaning of mathematical structures, but it is actually more abstract than addition and subtraction with carrying and borrowing, which is the very thing it is supposed to make more meaningful. From my vantage point, with experience working with learning disabled and low-achieving student, it is easier to learn place value well after some of the basic computational skills have been mastered.

Concreteness can and has been used in teaching simple facts and computation directly. Concrete objects can be counted or manipulated as needed to solve immediate problems without ever stopping to deal with concepts or mathematical structures. This is a step closer to reality and is a more sensible approach for those students who cope less well with abstract underlying structure. Counting and computation can be achieved more expeditiously with this direct concrete approach.

In some computational activities, such as extracting a square root, it is difficult to effectively use concreteness as a learning facilitator. Here, for many children, there may be no meaningful purpose to be found for its application in reality, thus making its mastery much less likely. As curriculum items become increasingly abstract or less common in the day-to-day world, this use of concreteness in learning will be less available for use in teaching those items to an increasingly large group of students, and giving them space in the curriculum is questionable.

As I prepare this third edition, the content of math curricula is more controversial than it was when I prepared the first. Confounding the problem of deciding its content is the standards movement. At what grade level should the content be placed if a decision is reached as to what it should be? The November, 2001 issue of the *Phi Delta Kappan* contained a series of articles under the heading "The Math Wars." There are very different ideas as to what content should be placed where as well as to what the content should be (Jacob, B., 2001; Reys, R., 2001; Trafton, P., Reys, B., & Wasman, D., 2001). When the curricula are assigned rigidly to a grade, students are required to learn it there, ready or not. This has caused considerable consternation when it is found that very large percentage of students can't reach the standard. Standards placed at grade level are Procrustean. Curriculum-based assessment, on the other hand, requires that student be placed at a comfortable place on the curriculum where they are ready to learn. The standard needs to be determined for each student. For some it should be well above the standard assigned to the grade, but for many it will be somewhere below.

The conceptual structure of mathematics is an interesting curricular area, but it is inappropriate content for low-achieving learners. When it is more difficult than the thing it is being used to explain, it is of no value to these students.

Concreteness of presentation is important in facilitating learning arithmetic computational procedures. A concrete mode of presentation is helpful when introducing new facts or procedures. Concreteness is better used in introduction than in drill for mastery.

Word Problems

Thought problems or "word" problems pose extra difficulty in arithmetic instruction. The difficulty will be quite apart from that of computation. However, skill in computation will be a necessary but insufficient readiness base for dealing with the solution of thought problems. Additionally, the problems will be presented in print, so sufficient reading ability to recognize all the words in the problem is a readiness requirement. When the student has both the computational skill and the reading skill necessary to do the problem, he then must deal with the logical processes involved. Word problems rarely directly state which computational process should be performed. A student is far more likely to see a word problem of the form (a) than (b):

(a) If Joe is six feet tall and Fred is five feet tall, then how much shorter is Fred than Joe?
(b) What number is left if you subtract five from six?

In word problem situations students must identify a pattern or gain some insight from the printed discourse as to which computational procedure should be used. If skill at seeing these patterns and gaining these insights is to be attained, then teaching must be quite systematic. The computational and reading readiness stages must be in place and then the various patterns representing computational process introduced in concrete and meaningful situations. Once introduced, the problems should receive the same consideration of repetition for mastery as is needed for computational proficiency.

Chapter 6

INSTRUCTION WITH ASSESSMENT

Regular, direct assessment that is not used for assigning grades but for maintaining students at an appropriate instructional level must be an integral part of instruction. In order to keep the criterion scores constantly within the instructional range for individual students, the instructional materials used in any given classroom will vary markedly in difficulty and will require continual adjustment. The very work being performed should be used as the primarily instrument of assessment. In this way, assessment will of necessity be regular and direct.

Assessment should not be used to determine whether or not students have attained or surpassed some standard, but to determine where they are ably functioning on the curricular continuum and then identify what should be the aim of instruction next. Standards-based assessment tells virtually nothing instructionally useful. It is likely to be demoralizing to both students and teachers.

Curriculum-based assessment is instructional useful. It is basically the informal procedures teachers often use already, but with CBA, these procedures are incorporated in the routine of instructional activity. CBA is not used to give grades; it is used to insure those students are engaging in instructional activities that are at an appropriate level of difficulty. This chapter will give attention to the details of these informal procedures, and show how they are incorporated in instruction in a complementary and reinforcing manner. Assessment is all too often viewed as an entity distinct from instruction; however, it must relate to instruction in the most intimate way.

Reading with Assessment

The informal reading inventory is a widely used assessment procedure. In an earlier chapter, Emmett Betts was credited with formulating the details of and the rationale for the use of the informal reading inventory. It was in the description of the procedure that Betts discussed the nature of the independent, the instructional and the frustration reading levels. These remain foundation concepts in CBA. The two important reading levels which produce success and achievement are the independent and the instructional level. The two basic indexes needed to determine whether a student is reading at one or the other of these levels are the number of unknown words and the level of comprehension. Information on either of the indexes can be observed during routine reading activities in the elementary grades. The reading behavior of a student should be observed in this regard any time she or he reads aloud. If a student demonstrates word calling behavior in every sentence, or if she or he stumbles over, misidentifies, or can't identify at all, a word in every sentence; then the student is trying to read at a frustration level. If, however, any of this behavior appears only in every three or four sentences, the student is probably reading at an instructional level.

In the case of word calling behavior, students may have good phonic decoding skills. However, they may be so preoccupied with sounding out so many unfamiliar words that they are showing evidence that the reading material is too difficult for them and is at a frustration level.

Oral reading behaviors like the kinds discussed above, can provide good signals that the reading material meets or exceeds the instructional level limits. If it exceeds the limit, adjustment in difficulty need to be made immediately.

Oral reading behavior alone can provide solid evidence of reading material at a frustration level. However, even fluent oral reading does not necessarily indicate that it is appropriate. Comprehension of the material still needs checking. In silent reading activities, the level of comprehension should be checked to make sure that it is staying at or above the 70 to 75 percent level. In directed silent reading activities, questions are provided before or after a selection is read. These questions should be used in determining and maintaining the instructional reading level for individual students.

Betts described another level of difficulty, or more accurately a level of easiness. This is the level at which students can read independently and recreationally. They encounter unknown words infrequently and have near complete comprehension. They should encounter fewer than two percent unknown words (one new word in fifty). A comprehension check would show at least 90 percent comprehension. This level is also called the basal level. This is a measurement term which suggests the highest difficulty level on a task which can still be performed accurately and efficiently. All children need much opportunity to engage in independent level reading activities. In doing so, they gain skill and fluency in reading, and as important, they can learn to enjoy reading.

Routinely checking oral and silent reading behaviors in normal reading activities is the most direct use of the informal reading assessment. This information is available and should be used to tune the difficulty level of material to the needs of individual students. This is the most direct use of assessment and the information is routinely available.

This direct use of the informal reading inventory is a departure from the more common perceptions of its purpose. However, it is this direct use that Betts intended for the procedure. Commercially prepared informal reading inventories are increasingly popular. They have come to be used more like individually administered reading achievement tests. Betts intended the procedure for determining whether or not specific reading material was suited to specific students. The instructional reading material itself was the informal inventory.

It is useful to have an informal reading inventory that is constructed of well graded passages that are likely to represent the range of reading levels of students in a teacher's grade or classroom. This will be a wide range that becomes wider up the grades. These inventories can be used to estimate the reading level of a student so that reading material matching that level can be provided. This will mean that teachers need to assemble the range of reading material in their rooms so that this matching can be done. After the reading material is placed in the hands of the students, then the direct observation of the reading performance is necessary to make sure a good fit has been made. This direct check is important for students who are beginning readers up to about the third grade reading level. As reading skill increases the teacher can rely more on the estimates for fitting students to reading material. More will be said about grading the reading material itself.

To make an informal inventory, selections of 100 to 150 words are taken from each reading level from a basal reading series, or other graded literature. Usually about five or ten comprehension questions are prepared for each selection. Because of the variable readability encountered within books, it is a good idea to check the readability level of each passage. There are a number of simple readability checks available, but possibly the easiest to use are those that are part of most word processing programs. When the passages are typed up in an age appropriate format, it is simple to go to the "Tools" heading of the program. There the readability formula will be found along with the spelling and grammar checker. If the passage turns out to be out of the desired grade level, some straight forward editing can bring the difficulty in line.

Starting at what is adjudged to be an easy level, the students start reading the passages orally. As the passages are read, the oral reading errors are recorded, and the student answers the comprehension questions that follow each selection. The highest grade level passage on which students have fewer than 2 percent word errors and have at least 90 percent comprehension is judged to be the basal or independent reading level. The instructional level is indicated on the levels where the students make from 2 to 4 percent word errors and attain 70 to 75 percent comprehension. If the reading selections are taken from the basal reading series or literature in which the students being tested will be placed, then the use of the inventory is fairly direct. This is a good use of an informal inventory. It is a good procedure for locating initial instructional level placement for new students. The instrument is made up of the actual curricular material in which the student is to be placed.

If the inventory is made up of selections taken from a different reading series or is a commercially prepared "informal" reading inventory, then the use is quite indirect. The grade level for the selections read at the independent and instructional levels is basically all that can be gained from these types of inventories. However, this may be enough help for a good many students. For students with less reading skill than their average classmates the more direct approach is better.

Once the reading grade level of a student is determined it is often assumed that any reading material that matches this level will fit the student. Such is not always the case, however, particularly with students reading at primary grade levels. There is no assurance that the selections taken from one set of material will be equivalent to that of another at the same grade level. Readability estimates are only estimates. When a teacher administers the inventory, identifies the instructional reading level, then places the student in a book of the same designated level, the placement is certainly better than chance. However, the material can very considerably in difficulty to some children. At the primary grade reading levels, the best use of the inventory is direct. The selections should be taken from the books available for use with the student. The instructional level match is then made with the material to be used.

Spache (1976) pointed out that the readability within a book in a basal series can vary widely. Therefore, it is necessary to continually attend to the reading performance of a student once placement has been made. The most direct method is the routine observation of student reading behavior during regular reading activities, using the guidelines for determining oral reading errors and comprehension for an informal inventory. If a student is demonstrating frustration level behavior, the teacher can provide extra help necessary to get through the difficult spot or make an adjustment in the material being used.

Measuring comprehension is a necessary but often difficult part of determining the instructional reading level. Comprehension is usually measured by preparing comprehension questions for each selection on the informal reading inventory. The questions types that are often recommended measure such things as recall of detail, evaluation, inference and interpretation. However, not all passages lend themselves equally to the formulation of the same kinds of questions. My experience shows that reliable results can be obtained by increasing the number of questions that are formulated directly from sentences in the selection. Consistency in difficulty of comprehension questions and maximum reliability among all the selections can be maintained this way. This procedure is recommended because of the difficulty encountered in formulating comprehension question of the recommended types. Too often making questions of the recommended kind produces questions that are far more difficult than the passage warrants. Illustrations of reasonable questions are included in a later chapter.

Informal assessment of the instructional and independent reading levels usually requires oral reading to check word recognition or word identification. The informal reading inventory approaches have varied ways of determining oral reading errors. Also, using these rather complex scoring procedures reliably may require recording the test so that portions can be repeated to assure that all errors are identified and classified. Such scoring procedures are far too cumbersome and difficult to be of practical use for direct routine use of the procedure. For purposes of identifying material for use with a student, some types of word recognition errors are more significant. Since unknown and unfamiliar printed words most directly contribute to reading difficulty, errors that point them out are very important. Gross mispronunciation, substitutions (not simple substitutions of common words that do not affect meaning), hesitations, and refusals (words that a student will not attempt) are the principal indicators of unknown and unfamiliar words. Oral reading errors that indicate unfamiliar and unknown words, together with a reliable measure of comprehension, make informal assessment very helpful in evaluating reading material.

Betts (1946) pointed out that "vocabulary load is one of the most formidable barriers to reading." The percentage of words that can be unknown in a passage at the instructional level may seem rather small (2 to 4 percent). But remember, this may mean as many as one new word in every other sentence. Relatively few unknown and unidentifiable words have considerable impact on comprehension. Student will need assistance in dealing with such challenging material, but that is why it is called the instructional level.

The informal reading inventory approach is the most important procedure for the direct measurement in reading. It is the procedure to use for initial placement in reading materials, and for monitoring and maintaining students at an instructional reading level. However, children may have not acquired sufficient reading ability to read any connected discourse at an instructional level. In these instances, informal assessment may be only simple word recognition, using lists of words, graded in difficulty by their order of frequency of use in print.

If a student can identify only a few words or no words at all, then readiness levels should be determined. Checking the recognition of upper and lower case letters and basic concepts about print will come next. Does the student have a concept about how a word is represented in print?

If an instructional reading level cannot be found, but the student does recognize a few words, then those few words will constitute the basis for the preparation of appropriate instructional level reading material. If the words are selected from a reading series, the remaining unknown words from that series can be presented and repeated until the student has mastered sufficient vocabulary to read instructionally at that level. Methods of preparing reading material using this procedure are detailed in the next chapter.

In addition to attention to the types of oral reading errors and to measuring levels of comprehension, there is another class of behavioral indicators of frustration level reading. These are those that indicate the student is off-task. If students are distracted from a reading activity by virtually anything, if they are constantly out of their seats, staring into space or daydreaming, the difficulty level of the reading material being used should be examined and adjustments made.

The difficultly of oral reading is usually underestimated. This is especially true for students who are at beginning reading levels. The combined effort of attending to meaning while attempting to identify and produce unfamiliar words is very taxing. For this reason, comprehension should be checked after a student has had an opportunity to read silently the selection under question. Oral reading should be done after the student has had an opportunity to first read the passage silently, if it is less stressful.

Oral reading is often one of the most used reading activities in the primary grades. It should be used more carefully. Children who cannot read well orally or those children who are reading at a frustration level may feel a great deal of stress when required to read aloud. The personality range of children varies from shy to gregarious. Shy students may feel great apprehension when they are required to read orally. Teachers should be sensitive to the fear these students feel when required to perform in an oral reading situation. Such students, when repeatedly confronted with these stressful situations, develop negative learned responses to reading that resemble the worst blocking behavior demonstrated by severe stutterers. In the author's experience, when students with average and above average ability have severe disability in reading, the cause can often be traceable to bad experiences with oral reading. Shy, reticent children should not be required to read orally unless and until they have the confidence to do so. Certainly no student should be required to read orally before his peers unless the material is at her or his independent level or close to the instructional level.

Informal reading assessment both the direct and less direct approaches are the most useful assessment procedures for teachers. It is entirely within the teacher's control. It is low-stakes and it informs instruction. It is usable both formatively and summatively. Unlike the high-stakes, standards based tests it can guide instruction rather than demoralize or confuse.

Low-Stakes Reading Assessment in Middle and High Schools

In upper grade levels reading is not a content subject area. It is assumed that students bring sufficient reading skills to read the subject area texts provided in each curricular area. Textbook publishers do make an attempt to keep the readability level of their text books close to the average reading

Curriculum Based Assessment

Table 2
READING RANGE, GRADES 1-12

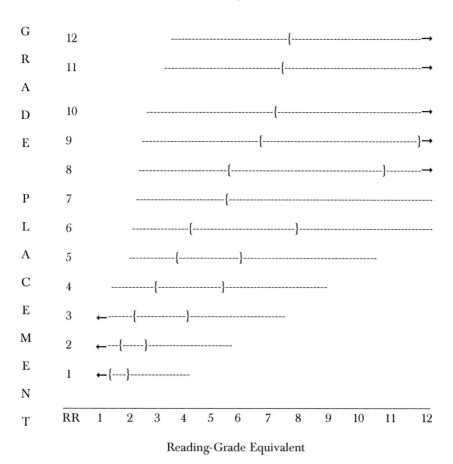

Reading-Grade Equivalent

NOTE: Students were tested between December and February. The space between braces at each grade indicates the reading level of the middle half of the class. At the first, second, and third grades, the range extends below the level of beginning reading into readiness levels. At the tenth, eleventh, and twelfth grades, more than a quarter of all students reached the test's ceiling score of 12-9. The range in each grade extends from the first to the 99th percentile, so the range includes 98 percent of the students in each grade nationally.

The data used to prepare this graphic were extracted from the 1998 Normative Update for the *Peabody Individual Achievement Test-Revised.*

ability level of students in the grade the books are intended for. However, the range in reading skills of the students in each grade varies greatly from this average. The graphic below shows the range of reading skills students in each grade from grades one through twelve.

Notice that the range in reading skills increases by more than a year each year. The ranges of reading skill illustrated on this graphic might seem extraordinarily wide, but it is factual. It shows what reading skill levels teachers are going to encounter regularly in their classrooms. Those students whose reading skill is at or above this average generally can read the texts and access their content. Those students who are not reading up to grade level are excluded from learning with their textbooks.

The graphic illustrates what reading at "grade level" really means. For many people this is a taste of reality that won't be palatable. There are as many students reading above grade level as are reading below grade level. Very few students are reading at the arithmetic mean of their grade. I hope it illustrates how difficult it is to keep students engaged in learning when their reading material is either much too hard, or occasionally much too easy.

Too often, middle school and high school teachers are not informed of the reading skill levels of their students. However, accurate information about the reading level of each of the students in their classrooms is exactly what they need if they are going to keep student engaged in reading and learning content. These teachers need low-stakes or informal means of gaining this information. However, the informal procedures for the elementary grades described earlier become unwieldy and time consuming because of the much larger numbers of students these teachers work with each day. Each class period brings an entirely new group of students, so each teacher may have from 100 to 150 students in their room every day. Administering an informal reading inventory to this many students is impractical, and since

there is little time spent reading orally the informal observation of reading behavior is not an option.

By middle school and high school students are reading
more words that they have never heard than words that they
have heard (Durrell, 1969). Consequently, the use of oral
reading to assess the instructional and independent reading
levels of students becomes unreliable. Students with good
phonic skills can pronounce words like *effulgence, mephitic,*
reticule, or *agitprop* credibly with no idea of what they mean.
On the other hand they may mispronounce words like *trage-*
dian, microscopy, telephony, or *facade* but comprehend them in
reading quite well. Reading assessment for instruction at the
secondary level needs to focus on the measurement of comprehension of words and/or text.

There are some low-stakes reading tests that can be quickly administered by teachers in their classrooms with little dis-
ruption. These are tests that are efficiently and expeditiously
administered and scored by computer. The STAR is a computerized reading test that gives a valid indication of students' instructional reading level, and it has an average
administration time of 13 minutes (see Buros, 2001, for a
review of STAR's technical characteristics). We have developed an informal computer administered inventory called
the Literacy Level Locator that has an average administration time of only five minutes. It also has a paper-and-pencil
form, easily scorable by hand, if no computer is available.
Both of these are low-stakes test that teachers can control and
use to inform instruction.

Assessment of Word-Identification Skills

The author has grown accustomed to using the term **word
identification** as the label of the skill used to identify unfamiliar printed words. Other common terms include **phonics,
decoding, word attack, word analysis,** and the like. Each
of these can be further sub classified resulting in terms like

grapheme-phoneme associations, letter-sound corre-spondence, structural-analysis skills, auditory blending, and **syllabication**. Some form of these skills are included most reading programs being marketed today. Despite some commonality in the labels used to describe these skills, what is included in the programs can vary markedly from one another. They are most different in the order in which they are presented and in which phonic skills are emphasized. Most of the elementary reading programs have the skill list-ed in a "scope-and-sequence chart" that shows which skills and in what order they are introduced. Some programs intro-duce and stress vowel sounds first. Others do the same with consonant sounds. Syllabication, consonant blends, accent or stress rules may receive varying amounts of attention at dif-ferent times and in different ways.

The variation and emphasis of these word identification sub skills means that assessment of the mastery of the skills should be specific to the reading program. This is necessary for test validity as was mentioned earlier, and it is also nec-essary to make sure that the word-identification skills being taught remain consistent with those emphasized in the read-ing program. The word-identification skill assessment should be of the skills being taught in the reading program. Tests come from a variety of sources. Some are specifically related to reading and are given to children who are having difficul-ty in reading up to grade level standards. Increasingly impor-tant as a source for tests, are National and state mandated "standards" or "proficiency" tests. These tests may contain their own scope and sequence of word-identification skills that are deemed important by consultants to the states. However, the scope and sequence of skills represented on these tests may vary greatly from what is being presented in individual reading programs across each state. Depending on the importance (how high the stakes) to the students, teach-ers, or the school system on its students passing such tests, it may be necessary to adopt the test as the basis for the word identification skill program. One can only hope that the test contains such skills as merit teaching.

When students do poorly on any such subskills test, they may receive an additional emphasis on the subskills missed on one of these tests. This emphasis becomes an additional, parallel curriculum. Teaching to the subskills deficiency dominates the reading instructional time. Learning useful word-identification skills is a helpful aid in learning to read, but a program that is dominated by them only dilutes the opportunity to read. Reading itself is the activity that must be most emphasized in order to make progress in reading. Word-identification subskills are not, per se, reading; though some see to actually believe this. Word-identification skill is only useful in learning to recognize words that are as yet unknown and in gaining the necessary real repetition of words that is required to become completely familiar with them.

Too often word-identification skill teaching is managed as if it were an isolated entity. The teaching of them occurs separately from the actual reading that is part of the program. Again, these subskills are useful only in the identification of words so that the necessary repetition of the words can reach a level required for mastery. The subskill teaching should be an integrated and intrinsic part of real reading activities, not a distinct and separate program.

As was mentioned previously, basal reading programs differ considerably in the scope and sequence of word-identification skills that they present. Those word-identification subskills that you are teaching should be tested. Each reading series has a scope and sequence of subskills that are presented over the course of their program. Most also have mastery tests that accompany them. Avoid testing students on comprehensive, even exhaustive lists of subskills. Tests that are intended to be all inclusive have been developed. The odds are that many students will miss some of these assumed subskills, and even though they have not been and are not being presented to the student, instructional time may be diverted to the supposed deficit. Instructional time for actual reading should not be relinquished. Remember, achievement in reading is directly related to time spent at reading.

Word-identification subskills are assessed in numerous ways. At times the testing procedure itself is more complex for some students than the subskill the item is intended to measure. For low-achieving and learning disabled students it is important to keep the assessment procedure simple and consistent. In subskill assessment several considerations must be influences. Are the skills to be tested in isolation or in context? On some tests letter-sound associations are assessed by asking the student to pronounce letters in isolation from words. However, children normally hear words, not fragmented sounds. The placement of letter-sound associations in nonsense syllables occurs on other tests. In still other tests, real words are used to present the letter-sound associations, but the words are isolated. Here, the context of the word is available but sentence context is not. Sentence context is necessary in providing clues to vowel sounds in words. For lower achieving students, the latter two levels, word context and sentence context, are preferable because the test format is direct enough to measure skill without being overly complex. These procedures are also more like the use of the subskills in real reading activity. The first two levels, isolated letters and letters in nonsense syllables and words are less like actual use.

With learning disabled and low achieving student, the simpler formats are better. They can be used to test word-identification skill in whatever curriculum or program is in use. The following examples offered to show a simple and direct form of assessment using real words.

For testing initial consonant sounds, a multiple choice of printed words is provided for each association to be checked. The following example is for the initial **w:**

rove   dove   wove   drove

All of the words in each row should be the same except for the beginning consonant. The printed forms should be new to the student. In each row the child is to mark the word beginning with the same sound that the teacher provides. The teacher would say, "Draw a line under the word that begins with the same sound as in **weed** and **west.**"

For final consonants, print a multiple choice of words for each association to be measured. The following example is for final **b:**

cup   cud   cub   cuff

The words in each row should be the same except for the final consonant sound. The teacher says, "Draw a line under the word that ends with the same sound that you hear at the end of **crib** and **rub.**"

Tests of initial and final consonant blends follow the same format. The following examples are for initial **spr-** and final **–dge**.

Train   stain   sprain   drain

Rink   risk   rid   ridge

In the first item the teacher says, "Draw a line under the word that begins with the same sound as **sprout** and **sprinkle.**" In the second item the teacher says, "Draw a line under the word that ends with the same sound as **fudge** and **dodge.**"

Vowels require a row of words that are alike except for the vowel sound being checked. The following example is for the short e sound:

speck   spike   spook   spoke

Two procedures can be used here. The simpler procedure is to say, "Draw a line under the word that you think is **speck.**" A more difficult one is to say, "Draw a line under the word that has the same vowel sound that you hear in **pest** and **hem**."

To test common syllables, the following types of items are used. These are examples for **–tion** and **com-**:

attended   attendant   attentive   attention

cemented   compute   candid   control

For the first example the teacher says, "Draw a line under the word that ends with the same sound as **action** and **mention**." For the second example the teacher says, "Draw a line under the word that begins with the same sound as **compare** and **compact**."

The format can be kept consistent for the assessment of most word-identification skills. It is simple enough to learn the procedure. Mastery of the subskills can be reliably checked using this format. However, word-identification skills can also be checked as they are used and taught in daily reading activities. Examples of how to prepare these activities are included in the next chapter.

The utility of the various phonics rules is quite variable. Only 18 of the 45 most commonly taught phonic generalizations can be accurately applied at least 75 percent of the time (Clymer, 1963/1996). In other words, if a rule is applicable 75 percent of the time, pupils applying it in decoding 20 words, would get the correct pronunciation on 15 of the 20 words. The vowel rules by far have the least utility. Consonants more consistently represent the same sounds, and have much greater utility than the vowels. Vowels are subject to dialect variation and can be confusing when the prescribed sound is different than the sound used in a student's dialect.

Beginning readers have been using consonants primarily since the first alphabetic writing appeared in Egypt some four thousand years ago. This alphabet was consonantal. It contained only consonants–no vowel letters. To this day the principle Semitic languages, including Arabic and Hebrew, are written with only consonants. Staunch advocates for teaching the sounds of vowels to beginning readers will find it hard to believe that English is one of those languages that can be read without the vowels. But as S. R. Fischer (2001) points out in *A History of Writing*:

> It is much easier for most languages to be read in consonants (top line) than vowels (bottom):
>
> W cn rd cnsnnts, bt nt vwls.
> E a ea ooa, u o oe.
>
> This is true for entire language families like Indo-European and Semitic. (p. 83)

Regardless how the reading program you use treats vowels, it is well to keep in mind the relative utility of vowels and consonants in word identification. I disagree with Francine Johnston's recommendation (Johnston, 2002): "I do believe that drawing attention children's attention to vowel patterns, not through lengthy rote drill, but through 10 to 20 minutes of daily word study activities, is both beneficial and engaging" (p. 216).

Richard Allington (2002) noted the relationship of time to the effectiveness of elementary reading instruction. Effective teachers devote more classroom time to reading. However, he noted that in many classrooms only twenty minutes of the reading period was spent actually reading and worse, many classrooms devote only twenty minutes of the entire school day to actual reading. This includes reading in science, social studies, math, and other subjects. In light of this, 10 to 20 minutes per day is a substantial amount of time to engage in reading in today's primary grades. I believe that any amount of time teaching vowel patterns in this restricted space is time not well spent.

Arithmetic Assessment

When a student gets about 80 percent of the problems or drill items correct on an activity, then that student is very likely meeting with sufficient success for it to be attention maintaining and to indicate that progress is being made. However, if the activity is structured so that even more of the items are correct, the practice gained may be more beneficial. Drill and practice are very much a part of arithmetic instruction. Repetition of each newly introduced item is necessary until the students gain familiarity and proficiency at it. Remember, a repetition of an item is only a good repetition or real practice that leads to proficiency, when it is done correctly. Missing items repeatedly can be negative practice. It is important to structure activities so that the students can get the correct answer each time the item appears. Accuracy at above 90 percent suggests that the repetition and practice being provided is leading to mastery of the items included on the activity. Remember that, in the end, it is only perfect practice that makes perfect.

Attention must be given to errors, so the fewer errors the teacher has to deal with, the less complicated instruction can be. When an error is noted, make sure the student sees the correct answer as soon as possible and additional practice provided as needed. A large part of what is called remedial instruction is devoted to removing error responses that have been learned through practice. At least ninety percent accuracy in arithmetic activities indicates that the practice that is going on is good, and that there will be little room for such negative practice.

Here again, the suggestion is made that all students should be getting the same scores on the work they are doing. It should be clear now that the scores children receive on their work are the primary guide to the appropriateness of the instructional activity. This appropriateness of fit is indicated by a fairly narrow band of scores. The arithmetic materials and activities used in a classroom should be varied considerably to fit the variability of the students in any classroom, and the index of having accomplished this is the uniformity of scores.

There are several levels of instructional activity in arithmetic. The initial level of instruction is when the new item is introduced. The practice that should follow immediately capitalizes on the short term memory of the student. The impression of a clear concrete illustration of the item sustains the student through the massed repetition of the item. If the student cannot successfully perform drill activities at this level, the introduction should be simplified or readiness for learning it should be checked and a lower level of instruction identified. The practice that follows provides for the acquisition of the item as it is nudged into the long term memory of the student. The next level provides practice for increased proficiency and fluency. The last level is mastery or automaticity. Students will vary considerably in the amount of repetition required to move through these levels. An important part of assessment becomes the attention to the amount of repetition required for mastery. Checks on speed and accuracy can be used to determine mastery of various arithmetic facts or algorithms. Even at mastery levels, fluency or speed of response is quite variable. Considerable leeway should be provided. It should be viewed in terms of the change in fluency from the time of introduction to the time of mastery. There is no absolute standard.

If a pattern of error has been established this response pattern must be corrected. Correcting error patterns is a remedial activity. Developmental work at an instructional level should produce skill without producing error patterns. However, these patterns may emerge because of a missing subskill, performing a wrong operation, or development of a faulty step in complex algorithms. Students; work should continually be monitored to prevent the recurrence of errors that permit error patterns to develop.

The following example should serve to illustrate a rather common pattern. A resource teacher was asked to help a student with subtraction. He just couldn't understand it. The child's regular classroom teacher couldn't fathom the type of mistakes the child seemed to make consistently. Given a set of computational activities in subtraction, the student produced these answers:

$$
\begin{array}{ccccc}
15 & 8 & 7 & 6 & 10 \\
\underline{-7} & \underline{-3} & \underline{-2} & \underline{-5} & \underline{-7} \\
15 & 8 & 7 & 6 & 10
\end{array}
$$

The resource teacher was baffled, so she asked the student to tell her how he was doing the problems. The student explained, "I'm doing exactly what my teacher said. If I take away the bottom number, what number will be left? Only the top one is, so I write it under the line." The errors shown above are the literal interpretation of insufficient instructions. The reason for the error is relatively simple in light of the explanation, but reasons are not always as apparent as this case shows. The most direct assessment procedure for determining the cause of an error pattern, if it is not readily apparent, is to ask the student how he or she is doing the problem.

The reader is well referred to Ashlock's (2002) *Error Patterns in Computation* for assistance in learning to identify error patterns so that remedial activities can be directed specifically to their elimination. The book is now in its eighth edition.

It takes almost as much time to learn an error pattern as it does to learn the correct pattern of response. However, the error pattern will require instructional time to eliminate, and then additional time will be needed to learn to do it correctly. These are additional reasons that scores on instructional activities in arithmetic should be kept quite high for all children. It not only insures success, but it also insures the instruction is efficient.

General Assessment

The bulk of the discussion of assessment has been devoted to reading and arithmetic. Other curricular areas do have special problems but the general guidelines for arithmetic or reading often apply. In teaching handwriting and spelling the same standards used for drill and practice in arithmetic can be applied. In various content subject areas, reading is the vehicle of instruction and so the difficulty of the reading material should be adjusted to within the instructional level guidelines. Beyond this, specific information is presented and is to be learned. Assessment should still be drawn directly from the instructional activity. Indirect means of assessment lose validity, and may become more difficult than the concept or content they are intended to assess.

Of all the curricular areas, the most difficult and subjective one is written expression. There are no simple standards represented by numbers or percentages here. I have attempted to impress upon the reader the great amount of individual variation that is to be found in academic ability in any classroom. If anything, this range of differences is even greater in language production skill. It is therefore necessary to find a reasonable starting point for each student where success can be attained and progress continued. In the same classroom successful written expression may range from only a one word response, to a query, to the ability to summarize rather complex events and even produce a short story. It is important to develop instructional objectives for students given these many different ability levels. The objectives should be formulated given where the student is starting, and then choosing the next more elaborate means of expression or simply just the next level of intelligibility. When a student attempts to write creatively and beyond refined means, papers should be edited only with the appropriate instructional objectives in mind. Students should always be reinforced for making these more elaborate attempts. An environment which fosters written expression is important. When students see their writing efforts covered with red marks, the effort is soon withdrawn. Assessment attention on these works should be directed to the students' progress on the limited set of objectives that they are likely to achieve and to which instruction is being directed.

Conclusion

The bulk of instructional assessment should not be used for giving grades. Grading is an issue that will be quite different from the routine of assessment and this topic will be the subject of a later chapter. Assessment's primary use should be in tuning the curriculum to the individual student's needs. Remember the ax and rack of Procrustus? Keep in mind that it should be directed to making adjustment in the curricular bed, not adjustments in students.

Chapter 7

THE PREPARATION AND SELECTION
OF MATERIALS

There is no particular method or approach to teaching advocated with curriculum-based assessment. The system should work compatibly with the various methods of teaching reading or math and even with approaches that are directed to different sensory modalities or learning styles. CBA is not a method in the conventional sense. However, CBA is a system of relating assessment to instruction. Regardless of method, it is a system of maintaining individual instructional levels in order to produce success. Consequently, it is also a system of individualizing instruction in that it matches the instructional difficulty of materials to the individual.

Direct Assessment

The most direct form of assessment occurs when the instructional material in use is itself used as the assessment device. This is so whether the assessment is for initial placement at an appropriate point on the curriculum, or is for the ongoing adjustment of material that is required as progress along the curriculum is made. However, for many students, their skill and achievement level may be so limited, that no instructional material can be found that matches their instructional needs. For these students, it is virtually impossible to find readily available instructional material that is suitable. In these cases, both the assessment procedure and the resultant instructional material will be reduced subdivisions of the more complex instructional material that is closest in difficulty on the curriculum sequence. Assessment and instruction then will be directed toward getting the students up to this entry level on the curriculum. For example, a new second-grade student is given passages to read from the primary levels of the basal reading program. Even at the preprimer level, the student can identify fewer than half the words. It is clear that even the lowest reading level available will be much too difficult for the student to use with success. The assessment procedure to use at this point is aimed at finding what word recognition skill the student does have with the basal vocabulary, so that a lower starting point can be identified. This starting point will be used to proceed to the mastery of a sufficient amount of the basal vocabulary so the student can read the preprimer at an appropriate instructional level. The student may be well behind the average for the grade, but will be succeeding and engaged not excluded from learning to read.

Remember, the focus of assessment is on strengths. Instructional activities must be comprised largely of things that are possible for the student to do. For children who have become curriculum casualties, it may be a challenge to find some strength or skill to use as a starting point; then given such a small base, it may be an additional challenge to prepare materials and activities that they can do. But it is quite possible to do so, and some simple methods of assessment and preparation of materials that have been used with these students will be illustrated shortly.

Teachers have grown increasingly dependent on published materials. For low-achieving students, however, it is often difficult to find published material that matches the needs at these lowest levels. This is particularly so as the students get older and their skill level is far behind. Now the problem is confounded by the lack of age appropriateness in the lower ability level of materials. When age-appropriate material is found, it often will not attend to the objectives of the specific curriculum in use. To make certain that the material is valid in regard to the curriculum and suitable for particular students, it is often of necessity, teacher made.

As reading skill increases, it will be more and more likely that conventional published material can be found that is instructionally appropriate. In addition, when a student reaches a high second grade or third grade reading level, it will be possible to find books that a student can read that are within the student's level of achievement. The matching approach can be more correlational and less direct.

Preparing Reading Material

Teachers feel most helpless when they encounter students for whom none of the available instructional material seems to work. "I just can't find anything for him to do." is a common complaint. Many teachers feel that it is beyond their expertise to prepare reading material if the "experts" who write all this wonderful stuff that works with the rest of the students cannot. The hard facts are that you are unlikely to find appropriate published material, and that you will very likely have to prepare a good deal of it yourself. The comforting facts are that it is possible to prepare it yourself and the task is not as formidable as it would seem.

The first task that needs to be done is to find what words, if any, a student has learned. Reading material that is comprised of mostly known words will need to be prepared using these words. The place most readily available to find known words is from among those words that make up the material that the student has been working in. Even though the student does not know enough words to read any material at anything other than a frustration level, the student may have learned to recognize some of the more concrete or frequently occurring ones. You may start with a list of high frequency words. One such list (Hargis, 1999) is included in the Appendix. Simply inventory the words that the student can recognize. With students who are still nonreaders regardless of their age, it is less frustrating for them to be tested from lists or flashcards. Since they have so little reading skill, they would not benefit from the use of context in identifying most of the words anyway. If the words are tested in isolation, the students will not need to be exposed to the painful process of trying to read frustration-level passages.

The number of words so identified may seem painfully small. There are other sources from which familiar words may be found, if the pool of words does not provide much to work with. Children may have learned to recognize the names of fast-food products, chain stores, and the signs and labels of commonly encountered items in their environment. They may recognize their own name and even the names of relatives and fellow students. Any additional words will be helpful in the preparation of beginning reading materials for these students. The following list of known words was identified with an eight-year-old student who had made little progress in reading:

> Preprimer: *a and big blue can for get go help I is it look me my red see the this to up we you*
> Primer: *he no on ran so too two yes*
> 1st grade: *of or*
> 2nd grade: *hot off*

With so few words to work with, it would seem nearly impossible to prepare any kind of reading selection let alone one written at an instructional level. However, it is possible, and it is not as difficult as it would seem from the alphabetical list of words from the four levels that are shown above. A more suggestive pattern of use can be made if the words are organized by part of speech and then placed in positions close to where they would occur in simple sentences:

a	Joe	can	get	me	and	big	for	yes
the	I		go	it	or	blue	to	so
this	it		help	you		hot	up	too
my	he		is			red	on	
	we		ran			two	of	
			see				off	

Notice that this student could not recognize any nouns other than his own name. This meant that some new words that were nouns would have to be introduced in the selections being prepared. The noun **bike** was introduced in the following selection.

> Joe sees a bike.
> I see the bike.
> Joe gets on the bike.
> I ran to the bike.
> I get on the bike, too.
> Joe is on the bike, and I am on the bike, too.
> We go on the bike.
> Joe gets off the bike.
> Joe helps me.
> Joe helps me.
> Joe helps me go on the bike.
> I can go on the bike, too.

The noun was introduced by providing a picture with the caption **bike** to go with the printed story. It was the only unknown word in the selection. This was the first selection that the student had ever read independently. He was surprised and delighted.

Notice that the word **bike** was repeated twelve times in the selection. By rereading the selection on this and subsequent days, the word will receive most, if not all of the repetition it requires for instant recognition.

In the next selection prepared for the student, two new words, the verb **read** and the noun **book**, were introduced.

Joe sees the book.
I see the book.
You see the book.
Joe gets the book.
Joe can read the book.
He reads the book.
You get the book.
You can read the book.
You read the book.
I get the book.
I can not read the book.
Joe helps me read the book.
You help me read the book.
You and Joe help me read the book.
We read and read.
I can read the book, too.

The word **read** received twelve repetitions in the selection and **book** fifteen. The words were introduced in a sentence written on the chalkboard. It said, "I can read a book." The word **read** was underlined in red, and **book** was underlined in **blue**. The words were underlined in these respective colors as they appeared in the selection. The use of colors were arbitrary and was used only in the beginning stages of working with the student to make certain that he could easily identify the unknown words in these selections.

You will notice that not nearly all of the words available for use in preparing these selections were used. Closer examination of the stories will suggest other ways they could have been written and other sentences that could have been added. Certainly, someone other than me could do a better job. However, these selections were prepared at the moment and put into immediate use to help a specific student begin reading independently for the first time.

It can be argued that the sentences are stilted; they are short and choppy; the word use is highly repetitive. Yes the selections are all those things and they are repetitive by intent. But, you must always keep in the forefront of your mind that the success of the student in reading this material is the foremost objective. It may be necessary to produce such material for extended periods until the student has achieved a sufficient and extensive word recognition vocabulary that enables reading with success in available published materials.

Practice makes it easier to prepare instructional level material for such students. Also, once such selections are prepared, they can be saved and edited for other students with similar needs. Even though a student has been in school for several years, it is possible for him to have learned to recognize almost no words with consistency. It is possible to prepare material with an even smaller stock of unfamiliar words than the previous sample. The fewer the number of words a student has in his word recognition vocabulary, the more the teacher will need to use repetition of those words that are familiar and will need to use nonlinguistic context.

The following selection was written for student who could recognize almost no words including his own name. The words **I** and **a** were used because the student recognized the names of these letters, and the names of the letters also represented these letters as words. The verb see was used as the new word and thus the verb in all the sentences in the selection.

I see a boy.
I see a bike.
I see a house.
I see a tree.
I see a dog.
I see a cat.

In this selection, the vertical alignment of the words provides clear visual indication of the similarity of the same word below it. All of the nouns were new, so in order to make their identification quite easy, their picture referent was placed beside each. The nouns introduced will have to be common concrete nouns that are easily pictured. It will be necessary to increase the number of such nouns that a student can recognize as well as the number of common verbs. Even a small stock of such words will make the job of preparing more interesting reading material much easier. As the stock of words is being repeated and added to, the following simple change to the above format can be added:

I see Ed.
Ed sees a boy.
Ed sees a bike.
Ed sees a house.
Ed sees a dog.
Ed sees a cat.

Add the student's name as the subject of an otherwise similar sentence frame. Pictures may be used with the list of nouns again, as needed. As subjects vary in the sentence frame, the inflectional forms of the verb will change. If the same verb is predictably used in the selection, the change in the subject will make the difference in inflected form more identifiable. More verbs are added in this way:

I ride a bus.
Ed rides a bus.
I ride a bike.
Ed rides a bike.

Irregular but important common verbs can be handled the same way:

Elsie is a girl.
Ed is a boy.
Joe is a boy.
Mary is a girl.
I am a boy.

The definite article, **the,** can be introduced in a predictable context. The introduction of the definite article will make the reading selections less like lists of independent sentences:

A boy has a bike.
The boy rides the bike.
The boy has a cat.
The boy has a dog.
The boy sees Joe.
Joe sees the boy.

The prepositions **in, on,** and **at** are common, important, and are helpful in varying simple sentence structure. These can be introduced in strong contexts to enhance their predictability. A picture can be used to illustrate the entire sentence to show the preposition in respect to its meaning:

A dog is in a house.
A cat is on the house.
A boy is on a bike.

The high frequency intransitive and transitive verbs should be introduced early. The action verbs **run, jump,** and **walk** are helpful. Adjectives such as **big, little, happy,** and **angry** as well as some color words can make the selections more interesting and easier to write. Past tense forms of the verbs can be introduced by simply changing the selections already used to past tense.

Only quite simple sentences can be prepared with such limited word lists, but that will be quite satisfactory for the time being. Remember, the student's success is the foremost objective, and the more success the student experiences the faster the stock of words will increase. Then the material can be more varied. With the few words introduced so far, selections such as the following can be prepared:

A boy had a dog.
The boy was in bed.

The dog jumped on the bed.
The dog licked the boy.
The dog ran.
The boy saw the dog.
The dog was happy.
The boy ran.
The boy was happy.

When a student's word recognition level approaches a hundred words, it becomes easier to prepare more interesting stories. The following two selections were prepared for such students.

The Three Bears

One day a boy was riding his bike in the woods. He was riding around in the woods for a long time. He could not find his way out of the woods.

He got off his bike and went up into a tree to see if he could see a way to get out of the woods. All he could see was lots of trees. He looked and he looked. Then he saw a little house behind some big trees.

The boy came down from the tree and went over to the house. He put his bike down by a big tree and went up to the house. Three new cars were by the house. One car was a red Firebird. One car was a yellow Corvette, and one car was a blue Camaro.

The boy went up to the house and knocked on the door. No one came to the door. He knocked and knocked on the door but no one came. No one came to the door, so the boy went to look at the cars.

He looked at the Firebird. He got in the Firebird, and what do you know? The keys were there. He could drive the car. The boy started the car and drove around the house. It was lots of fun. He had not been in a new Firebird before. Then he got in the Corvette. The keys were in the Corvette, too. He started the Corvette and drove it around and around the house. Boy was that fun! He went very fast in the Corvette. He went so fast that it got mud all over the house and the cars.

The boy was going to get in the Camaro next and drive it around and around the house, but then three bears came out of the woods.

The big bear looked at the mud on the Corvette and said, "Who has been driving my Corvette? They got mud all over it and all over the house, too."

The other big bear said, "Who has been driving my Firebird? Mud is all over my Firebird, too."

The little bear said, "I think I know who has been driving your cars. He is in my Camaro now."

The boy saw the three bears. He saw the three bears look at him. The boy's eyes got very big. He did not know what to do then. He was very scared of bears.

He looked over and saw his bike. He jumped out of the Camaro and ran over to his bike, got on, and went through the woods as fast as he could. He did not look back for a long time.

The three bears looked at each other and laughed. The little bear said, "We should not leave the keys in our cars." The big bears said yes to that. Then they washed their cars and the house. Then they went in the house and ate pizza and then went to bed.

The boy rode his bike as fast as he could away from the three bears. At last he got out of the woods and went home. He went to bed and had a dream about driving a new yellow Corvette.

The Boy, the Monkey, and the Vacuum Cleaner

One day a boy was going to his grandfather's house to get a vacuum cleaner. He was walking in the woods that were all the way from his house to Grandfather's house. The boy did not like to go to grandfather's house to get the vacuum cleaner, but he had to go there every day to get it. He got the vacuum cleaner to take home to vacuum his house. He had to vacuum his house every day. His mother made him vacuum the house every day or he did not get to see TV, and he got only bread to eat.

Every day after he got his house vacuumed, he took the vacuum cleaner back to grandfather's house. He had to do this every day. He did not like to vacuum and he did not like the vacuum cleaner at all.

He got to grandfather's house, got the vacuum cleaner, and was walking to his house. He was in the woods again. The boy was sad. His head was down, and so he did not see the monkey that was up in a tree that was by him.

The monkey had run away from a circus that day and was looking for a new home. The monkey did not want to be with the circus. It was not good for him to live at the circus. He looked down at the boy and said, "What is your name? What is that funny toy you have? Can I come and live with you?"

The boy jumped! He could not see who said this. He looked all around, but he did not see who said this.

The monkey laughed and said, "I am up in this tree. Look up here."

Then the boy looked up in the tree. He saw the monkey. He was happy to see a monkey up in the tree. He said, "My name is Jo. This is not a toy. It is a vacuum cleaner, but you can play with it. I do not like it. Yes, you can come and live with me. I would like that. You can live with me if my mother says it is O.K."

Then the boy said, "What is your name? Why do you want to come and live with me?"

The monkey said, "My name is Mo. It is no good to live in a circus. That is why I want to come and live with you."

Jo said, "O.K. come with me to my house. I like you, Mo. You are a funny monkey. It will be fun to live with you."

Mo and Jo, with the vacuum cleaner, walked to Jo's house. They went into the house. They looked for Jo's mother, but she was not there. Mo wanted to play with the vacuum cleaner. Jo ran the vacuum cleaner all around the house for Mo to see. He said to Mo, "See. This is how I play with the vacuum cleaner every day. I go all over the house with it."

Mo said, "That looks like fun. Let me play with the vacuum cleaner."

Jo said, "O.K. Go on and play with the vacuum cleaner.

So, Mo got the vacuum cleaner and was going all over the house with it. He said, "Jo, this is fun. A vacuum cleaner is a good toy. I like to play with it."

Jo's mother came into the house then. She saw the monkey run the vacuum around the house and her eyes got big. She said, "Look at that monkey run that vacuum! That monkey is good! I want that monkey to live in my house and vacuum. The monkey was very happy then. The boy was very happy then, too.

Mother looked at Jo and said, "Jo, we have a little house. You have a little bed. the monkey gets your bed. You will have to be in the car. We have to make this monkey happy. We want him to live here."

Jo was not happy about the bed, but Mo said that he did not like beds and that Jo could have it. Jo was happy then, and the monkey was happy, too. They liked to play and have fun, and Jo did not have to vacuum again.

As the student's stock of words increases in number, more direct attention can be given to introducing words that have the highest utility, a basal reader vocabulary, or the vocabulary of a book you would like him to read. When the student has become sufficiently familiar with enough words, he then can benefit from the instructional use of that material directly.

Lest the reader be discouraged about preparing material with limited vocabulary that is either interesting or engaging, remember Theodor Seuss Geisel, also known as Dr. Seuss. It was not until he was challenged to write a child's book with a 220-word primer vocabulary that he produced his best selling book, *The Cat in the Hat.* His subsequent books followed the same pattern of telling a story with the minimum number of words. The finest example in my opinion is *Green Eggs and Ham* which he wrote after Bennett Cerf challenged him to write one using 50 words or less (Reading Today, 2004).

Experience stories can be used with considerable benefit at the early level of instruction. The language will certainly be familiar to the student and these stories are much easier to prepare since the number of different printed words need not be as controlled. Also, it is often possible to introduce particular new words into activities that go into experience stories. When a student rereads the experience story, his familiarity with it makes the identification of the unfamiliar printed words much easier. The repetition derived from rereading experience stories is possibly the most important benefit derived from this activity.

Providing Adequate Repetition of Words

It extremely important to provide printed material that a child can read, but it is equally important to provide sufficient repetition of new words in this material so that progress is made in expanding his word recognition vocabulary. Gates's (1930) guidelines for repetition of words are fundamentally sound. Average students require about 35 repetitions of most words before they can recognize them instantly when they are beginning readers. Slower students require even more. Repetition of words can be achieved in several ways. In Dr. Seuss's books repetition is used to wonderful effect. In the selections illustrated above, multiple use of each word was necessary because there were so few known words to start with, but even so, multiple uses of words should be planned for systematically for slower students. These students are much less likely to get the incidental repetition of even those words with the highest general frequency of occurrence. Rereading activities provide an excellent source of repetition of words, and if there are several appearances of the same word in a selection, the student will benefit even more from the rereading. Written comprehension questions that are very simply and directly related to the selection can be used to repeat virtually all the words that occurred in the selection.

Listening to a recording of a selection while following its printed text is also an activity where the student can get considerable good additional repetition of a great many different words. The selection need not be made up of mostly recognized words, but the words in it should be unknown only in print. The student can listen and read along repeatedly until he has learned all of the selection and can recognize all of the words when presented with them in isolation. The more within text repetitions each word has, the fewer reading/listening repetitions the student will need to master the selection. The student will need some basic readiness skills to use this activity. He will have to understand the left-to-right, top-to-bottom tracking procedure required in reading. He will have to recognize what a word and its boundaries look like in print. Even then, the beginning reader may require some help and practice in keeping his place as he attempts to follow the text. Visual and auditory clues may be needed at first to assist the student with this activity. It is an activity in which a student who is far behind can catch up on a considerable amount of word recognition vocabulary in a less stressful way. One teacher varied this activity to capitalize on a student's repetitive listening of popular music. The student was permitted to listen to his favorite song as he memorized its printed lyrics. There were 67 different high frequency words that the student learned to recognize, and he did it willingly.

The selection for recording can be chosen because of its interest to the student or it may be chosen from a graded series of material. The selection should contain utilitarian vocabulary that will permit the student to read further, independently. These activities are helpful, supplementary sources of repetition. There is, however, no substitute for the constant opportunity to read at the independent and instructional level.

Remember; the thing that makes a real repetition of a word is its correct identification. The fact that a word appears, with the necessary frequency, before a student accounts for nothing unless he identifies it each time.

Skills Teaching

Curriculum-based assessment is normally neutral in regard to the method of instruction used. However, in the event that some method of instruction is an impediment to a student's achievement of success, some adjustment to this methodology should be considered.

There are many different word-identification programs in current use. They share one characteristic. For the less able students, they are frustrating and counterproductive. The source of this difficulty is the separation of the word-identification skill teaching activities from any actual reading. The reading activities and the subskill teaching are too often treated quite separately. There seems to be the general notion that there will be an automatic transfer of training to real reading once a subskill is learned. The fact is that isolated subskill training is likely to remain isolated and to be a subskill of nothing. The student will learn the subskill in the format of presentation, but not be able to apply them. The application of the subskill training must be basic to their teaching. Subskills taught from workbooks, games, and worksheets remain fragmented and abstract. They should be integrated with the selections the student is given to read. Subskills not directly applied in this way will not really be learned. If the opportunity to use them with the words that comprise the discourse being read is not planned, the transfer will not occur. The ability to use such subskills by the less able students needs successful practice as much as any other teaching.

Students will need to have appropriate instructional level reading material in which to practice these skills. New words in reasonably rich contexts are successfully identified using appropriate subskills. It is important to have this known context. Too often the student is expected to apply the subskills to identify an unreasonably large number of unknown words. But, the number of unknown words will reduce the benefit of context and place too large a burden on the student. More emphasis on subskills will not make the material any easier for the student. Remember; for success in the application of subskills it is necessary to effectively apply them. When children have trouble reading, there is always the danger that the reading program for them will become increasingly subskill centered. This means that more time will be devoted to learning the subskills in isolation. When this happens, there is no firm ground for rooting the skills teaching and no meaningful way to apply them.

A method of presenting subskills to these children, which insures the most success in their application, is called the "intrinsic method." The system was developed by Arthur Gates (1930). In it, the word-identification skills being taught are directed to words that make up the daily reading selections. The new words are presented in prereading activities which point out the letter-sound feature being taught and which aid in the identification of the new words. The subskills are also featured in activities that follow the selection, including the comprehension questions. Activities that combine comprehension exercise with word-identification skills can end most reading selections. Comprehension and word-identification should be meaningfully integrated. Remember; it is when there is an overemphasis on word-identification skills without the attention to comprehension,

that a student becomes a word-caller and does not comprehend what is read. The following examples show some
teacher-made comprehension activities that integrate word
identification. They were developed to accompany a short
reading selection.

1. What did the boy buy?
   a cap, a ball, a cat, a hat
2. Where did the cat have the kittens?
   under the bed, under the shed
3. Which kitten did the boy keep?
   Fatty, Blackie, Brownie, Puff
4. Where did the kitten sleep?
   on the box, on the bed

The comprehension of the story can be checked at the
same time that practice with word-identification skills is
given. The selection of the correct answer requires use of the
letter-sound associations that are varied specifically to provide this practice.

Transfer of training is not an issue here, because the exercise is related to an actual reading activity. The word-identification skills being practiced are on the words being introduced. Combining comprehension activities and the subskill
training fosters the active use of context and avoids the
development of word-calling behavior. Exercises can be
structured to focus on any word-identification skill in the curriculum: common syllables, spelling units, inflectional end-
ings as well as letter-sound associations.

Arithmetic Activities

No amount of repetition will guarantee learning something
if a student hasn't the counting concepts before the student
can add or subtract, and the student must be able to multiply
and subtract before long division can be learned. Mastery of
the constituent readiness subskills must be measured at each
step along the arithmetic curriculum.

Just as important as readiness is the fact that no amount of repetition will guarantee learning something unless the student gets it right at these repetitions. Remember, it is only a real or helpful repetition if the correct answer is linked with the problem. If a student is getting a wrong answer, the student is getting is getting a repetition of something that is incorrect. He is in fact a repetition closer to learning an error pattern.

A high level of accuracy is important in drill and practice activities in arithmetic. Only in this way can a teacher be assured that an activity is providing good repetition that leads toward mastery. A performance level of about 70 to 80 percent accuracy may be adequate for keeping a student on task, but 90 percent or better indicates that good repetition is being achieved, and there is much less opportunity to practice errors.

When a new fact or procedure is being introduced, it should be done as concretely as possible and then followed immediately by massed practice. Massed practice is where the newly introduced items are isolated and practiced. The concrete presentation will secure the item in short term memory for a sufficient length of time so that it can become increasingly embedded through subsequent drill activities. The initial presentation, which is then followed by isolated, will itself be subject to extended repetition for slower students.

How many new items can be introduced at one time? Miller's seven plus or minus two (1956) was discussed in an earlier chapter. With academically slower students, the number will be on the minus side. Miller did not include low achieving students in his study, so the number will be smaller than the five he suggested. Let's say that we are introducing the multiplication facts. How many new facts can we introduce and expect a student to remember long enough to benefit from the massed practice that follows? How many new facts can we introduce and expect a student to remember long enough to benefit from the massed practice that follows? A teacher will necessarily experiment to find this answer. The maximum number of new multiplication facts that can be introduced, with the student attaining at least a 90 percent accuracy rate on the massed practice that follows, is the level being sought. This level of accuracy on the practice activities shows that the student has kept the items in short term memory long enough to benefit from the repetition.

The initial repetition is provided through isolated drill with the new items being massed together. Subsequent repetition is spaced and mixed with previously introduced items that are being practiced for fluency and mastery.

Drill, practice repetition, rehearsal; whatever its name, it seems to have a bad reputation. Its careful management, however, is fundamental. It is where the problems which require remedial effort begin. The computer promises the technology for providing repetition as carefully as it is needed without quite so much time and effort in its preparation.

During the practice stages when addition and subtraction facts are being memorized, a variety of formats may be encountered. When the format goes from left to right it is called a sentence. Sentences for addition look like these:

$$6 + 3 = \underline{\qquad}, \text{ or } \underline{\qquad} + 3 = 9, \text{ and } 6 + \underline{\qquad} = 9$$

Sentences for subtraction look like these:

$$6 - 3 = \underline{\qquad}, \text{ or } \underline{\qquad} - 3 = 3, \text{ and } 6 - \underline{\qquad} = 3$$

The vertical form of notation $\begin{array}{r} 6 \\ +3 \\ \hline \end{array}$ for addition and $\begin{array}{r} 6 \\ -3 \\ \hline \end{array}$ for subtraction are also used in practice activities. In my experience, variation in format may pose more learning difficulties than the facts themselves. When the facts are at the practice stage I recommend that only one format be used. The only sentence form that should be used at first is $6 + 3 = \underline{\qquad}$ or

$6 - 3 =$ _____. The other forms can be very confusing. The symbols "-" or "+" will strongly suggest that subtraction or addition should be performed, but this will not be the case in the other sentence formats. The vertical form of notation will be used for virtually all the longer addition and subtraction problems. So, it seems a sensible way to begin. At any rate be consistent; don't introduce confusing variables at the practice stage with students who have learning problems.

Remedial Instruction

Instruction works best when it proceeds developmentally along the curriculum. When progress stops or goes awry, instruction becomes remedial if anything at all is done. Progress along the curriculum may be stopped because instruction is proceeding too quickly for some students, because of a readiness or skills deficiency, or because an error pattern has developed that impedes learning. The problem that is preventing progress will have to be identified, and then the problem itself will become the focus of instruction. The problem will become the curriculum. This will be necessarily so until the error pattern or skill deficit can be removed and normal progress for the individual student can resume. If the remedial program is not undertaken, there is the danger that the student will be further practicing his problem and thereby compounding it.

To avoid problems which require remedial attention it is important to make sure that success rates on instructional activities are quite high. This is good insurance that skills are emerging and error patterns are not. When errors appear that seem consistent, then some remedial attention action should be taken promptly. Remedial instruction is necessary, but it is replacing developmental instructional time.

When a student is clearly disabled by such problems, it may be necessary to review his performance diagnostically. There may be an array of problems that need attention. This leads to a major pitfall in remedial instruction—the overemphasis on deficits or problems.

When assessment is diagnostic, the diagnostician is looking for problems and deficits. When they are identified, a remedial program focusing on them will be prepared. This is fundamental to the diagnostic-prescriptive model. The pitfall is that a program focusing on deficits or problems can be frustrating and nonproductive. Remember; success should be emphasized even in remedial instruction. It is difficult to keep this in mind when the diagnostic effort is on problems and deficits.

When a remedial program is undertaken, it is just as necessary as ever to balance it heavily on the side of a student's strength. The ratio of knowns to unknowns should remain the same as for developmental instruction. The same levels of success and comprehension should be shown in the student's performance.

A secondary problem with remedial instruction is that it has the tendency to focus on isolated subskills. This is particularly true in reading. With low achieving students, on is likely to be disappointed if a transfer of training is expected from an isolated activity to actual reading performance.

Diagnostic tests should reflect the content of the curriculum in use. If deficits are identified that are not a part of that curriculum, the information may actually be trivial. Unfortunately, it is likely to receive remedial attention anyway. This will only dilute the time that is spent on the regular curriculum. This speaks to the importance of using content valid diagnostic measures, measures that are related to the student's regular curriculum.

Chapter 8

IDENTIFYING LEARNING DISABLED STUDENTS

The label, "learning disability," was first used by the late Sam Kirk (Hallahan & Kauffman, 1986) in 1963. It was an attempt to provide a unifying label for a myriad of terms associated with children who have difficulty learning. The many terms that are subsumed in this category imply some degree of brain abnormality and all imply a defect that resides within the student. The term learning disability focuses the attention on the learning problem rather than on the variety of confusing labels that implied some cause. However, even the label, learning disability, implies that something is wrong with the student, and that the cause of the learning problem is within him. Throughout this book, the curriculum, rather than the student, has been emphasized as the cause of most learning problems.

In many states, a discrepancy definition is used to determine if students can be classified as learning disabled. It has been concluded in these instances, that students can only be meaningfully classified as learning disabled, if there is a significant discrepancy between their capacity, or potential for learning, and their actual achievement. The size of this discrepancy is usually in the order of one standard deviation difference between potential and achievement. Sometimes the discrepancy is stated in terms of grade-years of achievement, depending on the age of the student. There are several reasons discrepancy has become popular in verifying the existence of a learning disability. It avoids the use of cause in the identification. There are so many subjective notions as to cause that confusion usually results. However, the main reason may be that a disability cannot really exist if it has not had a significant, negative impact on learning. It ultimately doesn't matter if the child demonstrates some symptom associated with learning disability, if he is achieving as well as he can.

My objection to discrepancy definitions of learning disability is that they require a student to fail to achieve for a sufficient length of time so that a discrepancy emerges. A student may have to endure considerable failure time before a significant discrepancy appears and some help provided. For many children who are simply low achievers, it can take several years of painful nonachievement.

Identification of Learning Disabled Students

Most students who get labeled as learning disabled are in fact quite normal. The cause of their problem is outside them; it is in the curriculum. Nonetheless, there are children whose problem does exist within them. They are a definite minority of the students with this label, but they need careful and differentiated attention.

In order to separate "real" learning disabled students from the far more common curriculum casualties, one must discover whether their particular behavior is the result of, or the cause of failure. To do this, it is necessary to provide instructional activity which is clearly within the students ability level and then observe the students' subsequent behavior.

When children do not have appropriate instructional-level material to engage their time, other behaviors appear. Certainly when a student is not engaged in the instructional activity he must be doing something else. A child who is unable to engage in the work of the classroom engages in off-task behavior. This behavior can take a variety of forms. It can range from quiet mental withdrawal to disruptive acting-out. The negative attitude that emerges may result in avoid-ance. Frustration-level materials do not permit sustained attention and give rise to such labels as "attention deficit" or "hyperdistractible."

Appropriate rates for introduction and repetition are the critical factors in permitting on-task and engaged time. Appropriate rates also permit success and comprehension. Success is reinforcing, and as Skinner (1972) pointed out, is enough reinforcement for most people. Material designed to facilitate correct response produces success.

The act of completing a task can be achieved when the activity is at an instructional level. Hewitt (1980) emphasized the motivation supplied by successful task completion. Success and task completion are the motivating results of providing material that is at an appropriate instructional level for individuals.

Appropriate instructional-level material is an essential, but possibly insufficient ingredient, for producing sufficient on-task behavior in "real" learning disabled children. These students have problems outside the curriculum.

The assessment procedure for identifying these students still requires providing them with carefully prepared instruc-tional-level materials. The student's behavior and perfor-mance is observed after the material or activity is provided. The observation may have to continue over an extended period while maintaining instruction at this level. Residual off-task behavior under this condition is evidence that the cause of the learning problem resides elsewhere, and must be dealt with specifically. However, whatever remedial action is taken, it does not lessen the need for providing appropriate instructional level activities for the student. It is counterpro-ductive to change off-task behavior when the task itself does not permit attention maintenance.

Thompson, Gickling, and Havertape (1983) reported on the effects of using curriculum-based assessment and instruc-tion with children that included a group that were receiving stimulant medication to control their behavior. This group of children was identified as having attention deficit disorders with hyperactivity. The group received both medication and no medication under regular curriculum conditions and under instructionally controlled curriculum conditions. The medication was either Dexedrine or Ritalin as prescribed by the child's physician. Under the no medication condition the children received a placebo in capsules identical to the regular medication. These researchers found that the controlled instructional level was as effective in maintaining on-task behavior as medication. However, the controlled instructional material had the positive effect of producing significantly greater task completion and comprehension.

Even when children demonstrate many symptoms or behaviors associated with extreme forms of learning disabilities, the primary intervention should be in providing appropriate instructional level material.

If a student's attention span does not extend to the time of normally assigned work periods, usually twenty to fifty minutes; the work should be shortened so that the task is within his range of attention. The student needs to experience the reinforcement provided by task completion. After the student has had consistent experience with task-completion the work periods can be extended.

The attention problem of some students may result from extra sensitivity to distraction. This sensitivity should be managed initially by changing the instructional environment to reduce distraction to within the student's tolerance threshold. Study carrels, quiet areas, or sound proofing may be needed to provide an environment that permits task completion. At this point, the student's toleration level may be gradually increased to more normal levels.

It is necessary to separate the real learning disabled students from the curriculum casualties so that an appropriate instructional decision can be made. In all cases it is necessary to provide to the instructional level needs of the individual students, but it is also necessary to determine if there is a cause outside the curriculum. The assessment procedure required will be automatic if instructional needs are being met. The residual off-task behaviors suggest further attention is necessary. In some instances the behavior itself must become the focus of curricular attention. In other cases the cause itself may need to be found. For example, a student who is chronically hungry is unlikely to attend well even under optimal instructional conditions. In this case the primary intervention will have to be something like a sandwich. Lack of sleep, allergies and other chronic health problems will also need a noncurricular intervention.

Which Approach?

In most cases the curriculum mismatch is the root cause of learning disabilities. However, a student's learning problem may to some extent be within the student, or may exist somewhere in the out-of-school environment. Nevertheless, regardless of where the cause lies, the first approach is identifying and providing instructional level teaching. Doing this is not only necessary for adequate achievement to begin, but it is also the necessary basis for the next level of assessment –the observation of behavior at the instructional level. Remaining off-task behavior suggests that the behavior itself will need curricular attention, or that you must look elsewhere for a cause to alleviate.

When students have spent some length of time at school without making much progress, they will have had plenty of opportunity to practice errors and develop bad habits. With these students, an effort to remediate these problems may be necessary as the first order of work. These problems may so permeate the student's performance, that any attempt at regular curricular work would only provide further error practice.

Remember, remedial work requires the same attention to instructional level as does the regular curriculum. A diagnostic-prescriptive approach is in order, but it should be balanced with the assessment of skills. Diagnosis implies identification of problems and deficits. This is important; but since success at the remedial activity is as important as it is with a developmental approach, the focus should remain on the student's strengths. Finding academic strengths with many students requires more careful assessment than finding problems. Avoid the diagnostic-prescriptive pitfall of assessing and focusing on problems and errors. It can frustrate a student even more.

These then are the approaches to dealing with learning disabled students. They include the approaches that focus on the regular curriculum, either developmental or remedial, or both. They include the approaches that attend to cause. If the student's problem is one of attention and distraction that remain after the first has been implemented, then a curriculum that attends to managing the behavior is appropriate. Finally, the last approach is directed at finding and eliminating or ameliorating the cause of learning disabilities which include a variety of possible health or social problems.

Chapter 9

OTHER ASSESSMENT CONCERNS

Throughout this monograph a link between the curriculum and assessment has been encouraged. When a test is drawn from the curriculum being used, maximum test validity can result. A student's progress along the curriculum can be plotted, since the test will reveal what, on the curriculum, has been learned. A student's success can be planned if instruction itself is used as a form of assessment. Performance on all routine instructional activities should be used as primary assessment information. Materials and activities are adjusted so that the scores produced fluctuate within the range indicating the instructional level. Of course this assumes that students can work at any place on a curriculum hierarchy where they can engage successfully. A barrier to doing this occurs when each curricular area is segmented and apportioned to grades; thereby limiting access to levels either above or below students' grade level placement.

CBA emphasizes instruction as testing. This should be the dominating form of educational assessment. However, teachers will necessarily deal with a variety of other tests and assessment issues.

Testing in General

A substantial amount of the school year is devoted to testing. Hearing and vision tests are routinely given usually in the primary grades. A variety of norm-referenced and standards-based tests are routinely given now. Readiness tests are administered during the kindergarten year. Some of the testing is called "high-stakes testing" because they are used to determine promotion from grade to grade and then graduation. It is high stakes for the schools and teachers when their students' performance is used to evaluate them.

Teachers give lots of tests in order to give grades. It the students do poor and failing work, they may be getting diagnostic tests, and possibly individual IQ tests. Typically, a lot of testing goes on during the school year.

Testing for giving grades is not often useful it is just something that teachers must manage. It seems to have little relevance to the instruction they are providing in the classroom. The high-stakes tests motivate teachers to modify their teaching activities toward their content. From the students' perspective, the tests label them, grade them, or permit them to graduate.

Standards-Based Tests

Of the tests currently used, the standards-based tests have the most direct impact on students. The importance of the tests is clear. If you don't pass the test, you won't be promoted or you won't graduate.

For some low achieving and even mildly handicapped students, the test can provide a new opportunity. If they can pass, it is possible for them to graduate from high school with a regular diploma, rather than something like a certificate of attendance. For these students, the tests' form the content of much of their curriculum. This is true if the standards set are at a level of difficulty that is within reasonable reach of the students. Notwithstanding this potential opportunity, the standards being adopted and the tests derived from them tend to be punitive rather than helpful for this group of students. This concern led the Board of Directors for the Council on Exceptional Children to issue a policy statement on the use of high-stakes tests (*CEC Today*, July-August-

September, 2004). The concerns expressed in the following statement: "Several examples of potentially negative outcomes include: higher dropout rates among students with exceptionalities; lower self-esteem resulting from repeated failures on exit exams; increased grade retention; lowered standards and limited curricula options; inappropriate emphasis on "teaching to the test"; decrease in the number of students with disabilities receiving a standard high school diploma; increased use of alternative diplomas that may limit post-secondary education and employment opportunities; and increased dissatisfaction of parents and increased conflicts between parents and schools" (p. 4).

Sometimes setting standards seems to be based on wishful thinking. Standards are usually set by "informed professional judgment" in each curricular area. Thinking that by setting high standards uniform high achievement will follow. Setting them high results in disappointment for the majority of students. When tests based on "high standards" are administered, the results are controversial; the tests are deemed defective, and the results must be amended.

Standards are not really standard. There is very little agreement as to what should be taught and when. Even in math there is no consensus. The November 2001 issue of *Phi Delta Kappan* had three articles under the heading: "The Math Wars" (Reys, R., 2001; Trafton, P., Reys, B., & Wasman, W., 2001; Jacob, B., 2001). Further, no one knows why we teach certain material a specific grade levels (Zenger, W., & Zenger, S., 2002). Trial and error and tradition are my guess.

Informed professional judgment as to what should be included in reading curricula is quite divergent and consequently the standards and their tests diverge as well. This divergence was described in a comprehensive study conducted by Donald Hammill (2004) titled: "What We Know about the Correlates of Reading."

The most problematic aspect of setting standards occurs when they are set too high. In this case too many students fail, are retained, or drop out. If they are set at a level above which two-thirds of the students can perform, there will be an outcry that they are set too low. This was the criticism resulting from a study done by Achieve, a nonprofit organization created by state governors and business leaders. It analyzed high school exit exams in mathematics and language arts from six states, and the writing tests from four of these states. The study was reported in an article in the *New York Times* (www.nytimes.com) titled: "Study Finds Senior Exams Are Too Basic" (Schemo, D., June 10, 2004).

Standards cannot be set at grade levels for heterogeneous groups of students without the above mentioned controversy. Standards can reasonably be set for individual students when their current skill level is identified. The standard then will be set at the next developmental step on the curricular hierarchy without regard to its grade level assignment. The standard for some students will be well below what is assigned to their age or grade, and for some it will be well above.

The "No Child Left Behind" law may have some of these effects. If the tests developed to meet the requirements of NCLB, become the curriculum for the grades at which they are administered, students who can perform more ably will be measured as advanced achievers. However, the standards to which they should be aiming may not be achievable because they are not being taught to. Their achievement will be squelched due to lack of opportunity.

Remember, skills and aptitudes vary greatly with each chronological age group of children, and that range of variation gets greater as each group gets older. The reading skill levels (the benchmark academic skill) of the average group of first grade students is about four years, from beginning kindergarten to fourth grade. By the time they reach the eighth grade, the range goes from mid second grade to the ceiling of most tests, twelfth grade plus. The range has increased from about four grade levels to over ten. It is not possible to set useful standards for nonstandard students.

Purposes of Tests

Tests can have useful purposes, if their content is worth teaching to, and if what they provide is acted on. One important purpose would be to avoid failure. Tests can determine if a child is ready to begin reading instruction or to move to a more advanced area of study. A second purpose would be to determine the causes of learning problems. These include organic causes, such as hearing and vision problems, as well as curricular difficulties. These causes, if identified, can be controlled or eliminated. Determining cause requires a variety of assessment devices, but many are in regular use. A third purpose is accountability. Tests that are valid measures of achievement are needed for this. Information from these can be used to evaluate the effectiveness of a teaching method, some new materials, a curriculum, an individual teacher of a school. Tests for accountability must be used formatively and summatively. Progress is accurately measured only if you know the level of achievement of individual students at the beginning. Significant gains in achievement or lack thereof won't be determined if accountability testing is not done this way. The tests must have sufficient curricular range so that baseline achievement can be determined in both the lowest and highest achievers.

The purposes of assessment described in the previous paragraph are appropriate to curriculum-based assessment, and they are an important part of it. However, most testing should be directly related to ongoing instruction, drawn from the curriculum itself. Testing is done through direct observation of performance on the daily activities that are used to reach curricular goals.

Avoiding failure was listed as a purpose with primary importance. Certainly the time to prevent a student's failure is before instruction starts. Americans seem to be in a great rush to start instruction, and once it is begun every effort is made to force students up to grade level standards. The unfortunate result of these practices is the failure of a large number of children.

The measurement of readiness for beginning first grade is important. Actually, it is the lack of readiness that is most important and this information is what needs attention. There are a number of ways this information can be used. A delay in admission to the first grade may be appropriate. This delay could range from a few months to even a year or more. Some children will simply benefit from the time to mature, while others will gain from the extension of readiness activities or the acculturation process that can occur given the extra time.

Reading-readiness tests have received criticism for their imprecision in predicting reading achievement. Their correlation with reading achievement level at the end of first grade is not particularly great. However accuracy in predicting level of achievement should not be considered their main use. The most important use of these tests is to identify children who are likely to fail. Most standardized readiness tests do this with considerable accuracy, identifying 80 percent of the children who are not ready.

When using a standardized readiness test, the information gained from it should be tempered by teacher judgment. Some children will fail in school because of factors other than abilities sampled by such tests. Teacher judgment along with information on the child's health and family background may be the only means of identifying potential failure.

Low scores on readiness tests should direct attention to other assessment procedures. If hearing and vision testing are not generally required, they should at least be available for those children who show a deficit in readiness.

Program evaluation and accountability needs to be a part of the teaching and testing process. Students' progress should be measured with quality standardized achievement tests that a sufficient range of difficulty so that the full range of achievement in every class can be identified. Too many tests have a limited range and so produce floor and ceiling scores that tell nothing useful.

It is always important to measure progress along the particular curriculum in use, but the curriculum itself should receive evaluation. Is it a limiting factor in achievement? You also need instruments which represent a broader view of achievement to insure accountability.

Grading

One of the main assessment activities seems to be grading students. Like eggs, they are graded with A's, B's, and C's. They are held against a standard; one based on their curriculum. The system is no problem for the students who get acceptably high grades, but it is a system that produces failure in a large percentage of our school-age population. It is a system that reinforces the continuation of the lock-step curriculum. Teachers expect some students to get bad grades. We have even developed the misguided notion that hard grading is good teaching and that too many good grades is "grade inflation." The grading system is a measure of the fit of students to the curriculum they are working in. It contributes to the failure of students to graduate from high school.

Failing grades mean that there is a mismatch between the curriculum and student. It really means a failure in the system. Our system should be providing an opportunity to achieve to the individual potential of all students. We must remember that the best measure of good teaching is the good performance of the students, and performance should always be judged by where the student's achievement started, not by their grade placement.

The success of a school system is marked by the success of all its students. Failure is more than just the opposite of success; it means that little achievement is being made. Failure is not only unproductive in regard to achievement; it has many negative behavioral consequences as well.

Success is not produced by simply accepting a lower standard for the same work. Success is produced when material and instructional activity is provided that permits a high level of performance. Giving a passing grade to a student on a math assignment when half the items are wrong is not an acceptable practice.

Scores on assignments and tests should be used to gauge the accuracy of the match that has been made. Remember, it takes a high performance level to indicate the match. Curriculum level and the material provided to teach it should be adjusted to produce the higher performance levels. All students benefit where this kind of instruction is going on.

The concern then arises that grades wouldn't mean anything. Everyone would be getting the same grades. My comment in return is that failing grades only mean that our system is imposing failure on some students. This failure should be viewed as failing on the part of the system. The only measured performance that really means anything is the actual level of achievement a student has attained. Grades don't tell this. Most grades should be replaced by substantive evidence of what the student is currently able to do on the curriculum and of performance on content valid achievement tests.

The mark of good teaching, and the best indication that optimum progress is being made by all the students in a classroom, is that student performance is at similar high level on all the work done. I am critical of teaching that produces a great dispersion of grades and scores. This means that little attention is being given to the individual differences of the students.

When testing is used effectively in instruction, it is not used to produce grades. It is used to continually maintain the instructional level of the materials and activities being provided. This means that the instructional materials are adjusted to produce the scores that indicate the instructional level has been reached. Since the instructional activity itself is the test, it is like changing the test to get the desired score.

Accuracy in matching instruction to students is indicated by the instructional level scores they are receiving. Even though the performance level is the same, the curricular objectives for the students in any given classroom will range over several grade levels. It would be a grand improvement if curriculum items were not sequenced by grade levels. It adds to the inclination to expect all students in an age and grade to be working on the same curricular objectives. Simply sequencing the items on a curriculum without regard to grade or age would lend support to the idea that students could proceed at their own pace. They would be less likely to be forced into a curricular lock-step with age and grade peers.

If the scores being produced are all in close proximity, it is very difficult to give grades. In the public schools, the elimination of most grades would be no great loss. Achievement is better reported by giving specific information on what curricular objectives the student is working, or by standardized achievement scores. In the latter case, if parents insist on comparative information, a student's performance can be compared with others in her or his age group or grade more accurately and more meaningfully than with the grades.

Should grades ever be given, or tests used, to discriminate? Yes, both should occur. These tests should be authentic and substantive. Some professions, trades, and crafts already require such tests. Such tests are necessary to determine if the skill is sufficient to let the person practice their trade. Nevertheless, children in the public schools should receive instruction that matches their individual needs in order to reach whatever their academic potential is. The public schools need to give each student the best possible start. Grades or discriminating measures should then be used by the professions' trades' and crafts to make sure that only the competent be turned loose on the public.

Chapter 10

ADMINISTRATIVE SUPPORT FOR CBA

Group Instruction

There is an almost overwhelming tendency to provide instruction in groups. We group everything; we may call it tracking or grading, but its purpose is to deliver a single level of instruction. If some students don't quite fit, we just haven't grouped well enough. We seem to think something is very wrong if we can't teach the same thing to the whole class. Our one-room, ungraded schools of the past, though there are still a few hundred functioning, are out of sight and mind. We tend to ever larger consolidations, so that we can place students in ever more similar age and ability compartments.

Individualized instruction is also considered within our need for group structure. When individual instruction is planned, it is aimed at giving some students special attention on the subject the whole class is working on. It is not typically aimed at providing instruction at a student's appropriate individual place on the curriculum.

Remedial instruction also concerns our need for grouping. It is aimed at giving some students special attention on the subject the whole class is working on. It is not typically aimed at helping a student work up to his potential.

Over the years interest in ungraded schools and multi-age classrooms ebbs and flows. In the case of "ungrading' it had more to do with architectural changes–"open spaces" than the delivery of multi levels of instruction. The physical

133

changes could not hide the fact that the same old forms of grouping were going on.

Some grouping is necessary, but we must shake the idea that grouping can somehow eliminate the need to provide for different levels of instruction in the same room.

The need for grouping results also from the symbiosis between curricula and the commercially prepared program that are adopted to serve them. It is difficult to say which comes first now. When a school system selects a math or reading program for example, it is also selecting its curriculum. The material provided in the commercial programs is designed for "average" students in each grade. They present day-by-day, week-by-week, and year-by-year instructional activities and materials that the average student can learn with that pace. We attempt to group students so that they will fit the layout and keep the pace dictated by commercially prepared material. The format of instruction dictated by these programs is single-level, group instruction.

Taking Control of the Curriculum

Commercially prepared, developmental programs hold a sanctified position, and have a virtual lock on the curriculum in most elementary schools. Granted, they do well for the "average" student, and they are very helpful in providing to the needs of teachers. However, they should not be held in such esteem. For students who can't meet their normative standards, they cause failure.

Curricula should be assigned to individual students not groups and grades. "Falling behind" and "catching up" are phrases that suggest a student has a problem keeping pace with his group or grade level. When, and if, those expressions should be applied, they should be only in regard to a student's own potential. Progress should be charted by plotting his or her progress along the sequence of curricular objectives. Progress should not be gauged by comparing students with normative curricular standards.

In order to break down the lock-step nature of the curriculum, the sequence of objectives it contains should be separated from grade levels and average pace of instruction. Instead of placing one level of instructional material in a classroom, several levels, that actually match students' instructional needs, should be placed there. The materials should be organized, not by grade levels, but according to the objectives for individual students in each grade. The reorganization of materials according to individual levels, rather than grade levels, would do far more to improve individualized instruction than any architectural change ever could. Edward W. Dolch described his rationale and method for changing from group reading methods to individualized reading in two classic articles that were his last: "Individualized vs. Group Reading" (Dolch, 1961, 1962). The reader is well recommended to them.

Record Keeping

If the curriculum is assigned to individual students, and teaching material is available to cover a wide range of instructional levels; then a method of record keeping that matches the two is necessary. Progress for individual students will need to be plotted along the list of curricular objectives for each subject area. The record keeping procedures should relate curricular progress to the instructional materials that relate to each objective.

Progress along the curriculum is noted by what has been mastered as well as what is being learned. This procedure not only is used to insure that the match between student and instructional material is being made, but it is also the essential information for meaningful reports of pupil progress. What a student is working on and what they have mastered is the most meaningful information that can be provided to a parent or to another teacher.

CBA demands that scores on routine tests and performance on daily activities indicate a good match between student and instruction has been made. Consequently, scores produced by instructional activity will be in the same ranges for all the students in the class. Scores alone, then, will not have meaning. They can only have meaning in regard to specific curricular objectives.

Standard record keeping is used for the purpose of attendance and assigning grades. CBA record keeping is used for maintaining an instructional match. When the record book for a group of students shows a wide range of scores and grades, it indicates that only a single level of instruction is available. The variation in scores and grades shows only how variable the students are in regard to this level of instruction. In CBA, the levels of instruction must vary in order to produce the same scores, which show that accurate matches have been made. The "standard" form of record keeping must change considerably to permit curriculum-based assessment.

Grading

In the previous section on record keeping, the problem with the conventional grading system was described. In fact, if curriculum-based assessment is implemented it is impossible to produce the variance in performance that is necessary to assign a range of grades. If the use of grades were continued, then all the grades would be close to the same. A teacher who used CBA, and continued reporting letter grades, would surely be accused of grade inflation.

Grades, in most places, should be replaced by a direct statement of curricular progress. If parents want to know how their child is doing relative to others in her or his class or age group, then the teacher can provide norm-referenced test scores, or compare the position of their child to others in his or her class on the sequence of curricular objectives.

Teacher Evaluation

If teacher evaluation were directed to the main components of CBA, it would naturally encourage CBA implementation. Effective teacher performance, in a classroom where CBA is used, requires a different standard than those typically used.

If a teacher is using CBA, the time spent in large group instruction will be reduced. Much more time will be spent in learning centers and in supervised study activities. Individual and small group activities will be going on simultaneously. Peer tutoring will be used commonly. The teacher will spend far less time in front of the class lecturing and demonstrating. The teacher's lesson plans will reflect multiple levels of activity. Lesson plans will be evaluate for attention to matching students to activities on their curricular skill level rather than for how well they conform to one prescribed level and delivery format.

The evaluation procedure for teachers needs to focus on the priorities of CBA. The first thing that should be determined is if there is an accurate match between instructional activity and student. Are the students being given work that they can do? Evidence for this can be gained from direct observation in the classroom and by examining classroom records. The behavior that suggests that the match has been made is time-on-task. Academically engaged time should be evident in all of the students. The records should show that the students are being given work that matches their achievement level. There should be no poor and failing grades.

Examination of work done by the students and observation of work being done will show a high level of performance and comprehension for all students. The work will be at a variety of levels, but performance will be similar. An evaluation procedure will be a part of the instructional activities.

Pupil progress should be checked, but progress should be checked in regard to what the student's achievement level was when she or he entered the teacher's room. Progress should be viewed in regard to eliminating discrepancies between achievement and potential for achievement. No teachers should feel penalized by having slow or handicapped students in their room. This is one cause of controversy and resistance to teacher evaluation based on student performance.

Testing Programs

There are means for determining the effectiveness of teachers and schools other than tests. Daily attendance is important. Students who feel secure and successful are better attenders. At the secondary level the dropout rate is an excellent indicator. If students experience success and achievement, they are far more likely to stay in school. Schools vary widely culturally and socioeconomically. A low dropout rate and high employment rate for graduate of one school are as important measures of effectiveness as high SAT scores with high college attendance are for another.

Some administrative policies on testing that would foster effectiveness in regard to the above, and promote CBA are: First, achievement test information should be used to insure that all students were provided instruction that matched their current level of performance. This would be only a general gauge to be sure, but it would encourage individual attention to students needs. Second, achievement gains from baseline performance of students. Teachers, schools, and students should be judged not from how high the achievement is now, but from how high it came from. Third, there should be a policy that directs teacher to make the routine assessment be used for matching students with instructional materials. If students are doing poorly on daily work, the time to act on this information is immediate. Finally, testing should not be used to evaluate students, teachers and schools against some grade level standard. The standard should always be based on gain.

The Individuals with Disabilities Education Act (IDEA) requires that handicapped students be educated with their nonhandicapped peers whenever practicable. Having a handicapped student placed in one's classroom has caused considerable anxiety in some regular classroom teachers. Actually, most mildly handicapped children are classed as learning disabled and do not have teaching or learning requirements that vary much from the lower achieving students who are already in the classroom. If a teacher is adequately managing the individual differences in her or his room, then the problem posed by these new students should not be particularly great.

As has been stressed all along, most mildly handicapped students are actually curriculum casualties. Their primary educational need is for appropriate instructional level placement. Teachers who are willing to accept these students and who have demonstrated the ability to provide to the range of instructional levels already in their classrooms, are candidates for taking handicapped students.

On the surface this may seem to be an imposition on those teachers who are doing good work. The ability to manage to teach to manage to teach to the different instructional levels of a classroom full of students is the most important characteristic of good teachers. In fact, these are the primary abilities of the master teacher. This ability should be the primary component of teacher evaluation, and when identified, it should be rewarded. So, as a form of reward, or merit pay, I would suggest that when a handicapped student is placed in this exceptional teacher's room, a salary bonus accompany the student. Both student and teacher would, in this way, benefit from this teacher's skill, and mainstreaming would not be considered a burden. It might go a long way in helping to make handicapped students become better accepted.

Summary

Curriculum-based assessment ultimately must be practiced by the individual classroom teacher, because it involves the routine of daily instruction. Nevertheless, there are some powerful administrative tools that can be applied to encourage its practice. If curricular material were distributed in multilevels as needed within classrooms, it would not only be readily available for use by the children that need it, but it would also legitimize the idea that it is alright to work at a variety of levels within one grade. A system of record keeping that showed the match between student instructional level and the actual level of instruction being provided would keep individual differences before the teachers' eyes, constantly. It would also require that a student's progress be reported by his own appropriate level of achievement progress. The practice of grading should be modified by using reports of progress and achievement in place of letter grades. The use of letter grades fosters single level instruction in order to produce a range of grades. This practice should be curtailed. Finally, teacher evaluation procedures that value the features of CBA would certainly encourage its implementation, and it certainly would do so if effective use of CBA were monetarily rewarded.

Chapter 11

TESTS AND THE CURRICULUM

Chicken or Egg

Does the adoption of a test lead to the development of a curriculum or does the adoption of a curriculum lead to the development of a test? Actually, either is a possibility. The national debate that concerns standards-based testing presumes that what will be tested is what will be taught.

Currently, all of the states are engaged in developing tests to measure achievement in the primary curricular areas. The tests will be administered annually according to the No Child Left Behind act. It is generally recognized when the tests are developed the substance of the curriculum is also chosen. It would be stupid to do otherwise. Suppose the tests measure things that are not taught or have not as yet been taught; the tests would reflect this and there would be great risk of looking incompetent. The tests administered at each grade will dictate much of the curriculum for that grade.

The fact of the relationship between a high-stakes achievement test and any curriculum is conceded. There is general recognition that we must determine what needs to be taught (curricular content) if we are to determine what is to be tested.

Teaching the Test

In coming to the recognition that there is this intimate relationship between test and curriculum—what is taught and

141

what is tested—we find ourselves in a position that contradicts a longstanding prejudice. The prejudice is that teaching the test is a bad practice.

It is an old prejudice, old beyond our recollection, but firmly held, and it colors virtually all our testing practices. Now as we are considering standards and standard-based testing across all the states, we appear to concede the relationship between what is taught and what is tested. Nonetheless, we feel the old prejudice.

The prejudice lives despite the knowledge that tests must be made up of the thing they are to measure if they are to be valid. This is a fundamentally important characteristic of a valid achievement test. This form of validity is called content validity.

The curriculum contains the items that are to be achieved. The tests contain items that measure their attainment. The tests must specifically measure things being taught in order to have content validity. We must test what we teach in order that we can have valid tests. Consequently we must teach what we test.

The biggest problem with standards-based tests that are assigned to each grade level is that it may not have any items below that grade or above that grade, absent the items, then absent the curricular content to represent them. These tests do not have content validity for students whose achievement is outside its range of sensitivity. Therefore, growth and achievement will not be assessed by them. Valid tests must have sufficient range above and below grade level to be sensitive to the full range of learning levels in the grade it is being used in. I view this as a huge problem.

The Tail Wagging the Dog

We have all too often let tests dictate what we teach without considering what it is they measure. This is done despite the afore mentioned prejudice. We have lots of tests. I have mentioned achievement tests. We have several nationally normed achievement tests that are widely used, and now we have many standards-based achievement tests developed at the state level. We also have tests to diagnose the reasons for lack of achievement. We have tests to determine when readiness for acceptable achievement might be expected.

When we give tests, we must presume their credibility. Surely they will reveal the true level of achievement, or the problems that prevent it. Whatever their results, then, we feel compelled to act accordingly. What the test results tell directly, or suggest through interpretation, must be considered for inclusion in the curriculum. Tests can direct us on what to teach, when to teach, and how to teach. We can only hope that what they are measuring is worth teaching or the guidance they are providing is worth following.

Certainly, diagnostic test results will lead to teaching those things that are revealed to be deficiencies. Teachers want their students to do better. Consequently, they will be influenced in what they are teaching by what the tests contain.

Tests influence what we teach. Indeed, tests may form the basis for the curriculum. In other words, the tail does often wag the dog.

Test and Curriculum Alignment

Teaching the test may be a pejorative expression, but it does label a common practice. We should be more reflective concerning this practice, however. Teaching the test need not be a pejorative expression. Remember the nature of content validity. Still, we need tests with content worth teaching to.

Tests and curricula may be selected independently. If it is done independently we are making the assumption that the tests are a kind of generic measure of achievement in each curricular area. Such is not often the case. Reading programs vary in the content, scope, and sequence of the skills they contain. Common achievement tests seldom adequately sample items from a specific curriculum. Tests that purport to diagnose reading problems measure attributes that are not part of the reading program in actual use with the students being tested. Some tests measure things that have only a marginal or even a dubious relationship with reading skill (Hammill, 2004). If the information from these tests is followed, there will be only marginal achievement gains in reading if there are any gains at all. We need to evaluate tests in regard to their content validity as well as the predictive validity of the test itself. Are the tests strongly related to reading achievement?

If we want content validity, if we want to measure how much of a curriculum has been learned, then the achievement test should be made up of an adequate sample of the items at each level of that curriculum. Curriculum content – what we want students to learn – should be identified first. The tests to measure progress in mastery of this content should be drawn from this content–the larger the sample drawn the better. This insures content validity. Tests developed in this way will accurately measure how well the teachers and schools do in imparting curricular objectives to their students.

Testing and teaching, teaching and testing, requires that both tests and curriculum be of the same material. Then the quality of teaching is monitored accurately, and problem areas can be accurately identified. If tests do drive the curriculum as was asserted earlier, then be advised: Choose your tests well; they will become your curriculum.

Curriculum-Referenced Testing

The problem with content validity of tests prompted the development of curriculum-based assessment (CBA) (Hargis, 1982, 1987; Tucker, 1985). It also prompted the development of curriculum-based measurement (CBM) (Shinn, 1989).

The primary characteristic of both of the assessment approaches is that they are curriculum referenced. The curriculum itself is the basis of assessment. Beyond this common point, CBM and CBA differ markedly (Hargis, 1993). The advocates of CBM depart from the form of CBA that I advocate on tow principle points. The first is that CBM is a norm-referenced system. The test items are drawn from the curriculum and then normative information is determined by administering the tests in specific locales and then using these data.

A basic assumption underlying CBM is that learning problems are defined as performance discrepancies. Significant performance discrepancies are shown by a small number of students who don't meet the "reasonable" expectations set in general education programs for their grade and age peers. The determination of these expectations and then the discrepancies from them require the development of empirical local norms. Learning problems are defined as a measured normative difference from reasonable expectations for a student's grade and age peers. The purpose of the CBM procedure is to close the gap between the actual performance of a student and his expected performance as determined by the norms gained from his age and grade peers.

I disagree in principle on this point. Norms established around our lock-step curricular and school organization distort the normal variation in learning and achievement rates that we should expect. Trying to force children to fit standards and expectations based on the lock-step curriculum organization of our schools is what has caused our problems already. This system produces the curriculum casualties I have alluded to elsewhere.

I argue that curricula should be fitted to students—not the reverse. This fitting of the curriculum to the student was a primary reason for developing criterion-referenced testing and later for the development of curriculum-based assessment. Students should be permitted to work at the highest step on the curriculum where they can perform as comfortably as their high achieving peers. This should be done without regard to expectations based on lock-step grade level norms.

With CBM, the measurement of performance discrepancies and the development of local norms become central activities. The end result of measurement becomes simple numerical description. It isolates assessment from instructional activity.

With CBA, assessment is not isolated from the instructional procedure. Assessment is used for immediate action and feedback. If a student's performance is observed to fall below appropriate instructional levels, the time to act is at that moment.

The primary objective of CBA is success. Measurement that is an intrinsic part of instruction is used to insure that instructional levels are always maintained. CBM does not consider instructional levels or success. The number of words read correctly per minute, the number of letters spelled correctly in a word, or correct numerical responses are passively charted and graphed. Rate of progress, or lack thereof, is examined at summative points and only then will the course of instructional activity be changed if progress appears unsatisfactory. The difficulty of a task and the failure and frustration of the student attempting to engage in it is only a matter to be charted in CBM. In CBA, this problem would require immediate action to insure the student could engage and succeed in the instructional activity.

With CBM, routine performance will be left to vary. It will be duly noted and recorded graphically. The instructional level metrics are not part of data collection. With CBA, the variation in performance levels is restricted by design instructional success levels.

Items for CBM tests and monitoring probes are drawn from the instructional material being used in the classroom. A routine monitoring measure for reading might be reading a list of words containing the phonics skill being taught at the time. A summative test would be reading orally a passage from the basal reader being used to check fluency. In the routine testing the number of words read correctly per minute is recorded and graphed to plot progress over time. With the oral reading test, the fluency rate per minute would be graphed each week over the school year.

In either of the above CBM procedures, identifying the instructional level is not a consideration. What is under consideration is the shape of the graph. Does the slope of the line indicate that there is an increase in the number of words correctly identified and is there an increase in fluency of oral reading. If after 10 or 12 weeks, there is little or no improvement toward the mean of the local norms, change in instructional method may be recommended.

CBA's method of assessment is less formal and is a part of instructional activity. It is not intrusive. Routine assessment is the observation of the students engaging in instructional activity. If their performance falls below the instructional level standard, or if the task is too hard to persist in without stress and frustration, the activity and materials are changed or modified to produce successful instructional level engagement.

Summative assessment over extended periods is used to chart progress along the curriculum hierarchy. Students are not permitted to fail or do poorly. The metric is used to adjust and match material and activity to the students in order to achieve the desired performance levels.

CBM measures are not concerned with measuring performance while engaged in learning activities. Students could be having to cope with frustratingly difficult , failure producing work. Measurement is done by means of probes; the results of which are used to graph change. Decisions about taking action only occur after extended periods of time and inspection of the graphs, during which time students may well be failing.

CBA is a continually active assessment process that is intrinsic to instruction. CBM is an intrusive measurement procedure that is isolated from instruction.

Chapter 12

MAKING SUCCESS THE BASIS OF ASSESSMENT

Generally, when asked about their experiences with tests and assessment, teachers reply that the testing that goes on in their schools is intrusive, disruptive, confusing, and that some of it is a chore done to grade students. I agree with their feelings. Measurement practices should change. My view is that most testing should be so much a natural part of instruction that it is not even considered a separate activity, let alone an intrusive one.

There should be curriculum based measures that place students at an entry point on the curriculum that represents their current readiness level and their achievement level. There also needs to be a means of identifying problems that are interfering with learning that is attuned to the curriculum in use. Finally, the students themselves should have the means to be engaged in self-assessment to monitor their own progress without apprehension.

Level of Entry

Level of instruction and grade level are the same in lock-step curriculum systems. Grade placement determines where instruction starts. The curriculum scope and sequence is assigned to each grade from kindergarten through the twelfth grade. Generally students are assigned to a grade according to their chronological age. With their chronological age

149

peers, the students are to partake of the curriculum offering according to their personal ability levels. The curriculum sequencing by grades produces the lock-step order. All students regardless of ability level must proceed through at the same pace fro the same starting point. At the beginning, in primary grades, teachers may organize their classes into ability groups, usually three, to manage the wide range of entry skills and learning rates that normally occur. Occasionally, schools will use "transition" classes which are an intermediate step between kindergarten and first grade, to hold students until they are a little more ready to join the lock-step march through the grade sequence.

Inevitably, when students are assigned to curricular slots, casualties occur. Variable students do not al fit rigidly proscribed slots in the lock-step. Curricular sequences and standards cannot be assigned to grades and then students to the grades without casualties. Curricular sequences must exist unrestricted by lock-steps of grades. Casualties are produced at both ends of the academic ability continuum; abject failure at the low end and failure to reach potential at the high end.

Measurement in education unwittingly focuses on the consequences of fitting students to the lock-step curriculum. It should focus on placing individual students at appropriate places on any curricular sequence. This point, or entry level, has several defining characteristics. It is the instructional level, or point at which a student can engage in learning comfortably and successfully. It defines the basal or baseline skill level of the student. It defines the fund of skills upon which subsequent instruction can build. It marks the current level of functioning or achievement. It provides benchmark points from which achievement gains and accountability measures may be taken.

Substantive information rather than normative scores should be the result of assessment. Specific information, the details of what a student can do, is necessary information for defining an entry point where progress can occur successfully. To illustrate this point, consider the following experience:

A group of adolescent boys who were in a classroom for learning disabled in a junior high school were included in a reading research project. The project was intended to check certain behaviors while the students were engaged in reading. It was necessary to determine the current level of reading achievement for each of the students. All of the students had received the same standardized achievement tests at a recent date and the grade equivalent scores in reading on each student were identified so that reading material with those readability levels could be matched with each of the boys.

The grade equivalent scores for the boys ranged from about 1.5 to little over 2.0. High interest low readability materials were selected with the range of readability demonstrated by these students. The books were provided to them and an informal check was performed to see if the match had been satisfactory.

Each student was to read orally from the book provided to see if it was within the instructional level range described by Emmett Betts (1946). It became immediately apparent that we had not accomplished this. None of the boys was able to read even half the words on the first page of their books!

It was apparent that grade equivalent scores from the test were not adequate in identifying a specific entry level where real reading could commence. It was apparent that we needed to look for a more sensitive and direct measure of reading ability if we were to find reading materials that the students could engage in.

It was through using actual reading instructional materials as informal reading tests that we found that the standardized tests were actually far less sensitive than this informal procedure. It subsequently became apparent through using this same informal procedure in checking the suitability of more

material that we would have to find still more specific, substantive measures if we were to find entry level reading material that these boys could actually engage in reading independently.

Since no reading material could be found in which any of
the students could engage successfully, it was decided that
such material, at the individual instructional reading levels of
the students would have to be composed for them. Since
instructional reading material must be composed of known
words–no more than one new word in 25–an inventory of
the words actually known by the students was undertaken.
The inventory list was made up of the high-frequency words
used in the books we started with. The list of words from
each book was administered as a sight word test to see which
and how many words could be recognized.

The words each student knew from these lists would
become the basis for composing and preparing instructional
level reading material. Whatever fund of known words each
student had would be used as the foundation vocabulary.
Unknown words from the same list would be introduced at a
2 to 4 percent level of the material. This was the plan.
However, the number of known words the boys could recognize was painfully small. The sight word vocabularies for
the boys ranged from about a dozen to something over forty
words. After more than six years in school, the boys were still
nonreaders.

A dozen words or even forty words is a very constricted
vocabulary for use in written composition, as we soon found.
We did, however, manage to produce reading material in
each case that was at an instructional level. With so few sight
words, it required being very repetitive with those few.
Literary impulses had to be checked. The preparation of
instructional level material and insuring student success was
paramount. The reading selections for students with the most
restricted vocabularies were, of course, the most repetitive
and had the most simple and constricted sentences. The

material was carefully prepared in regard to format. There was no large print and it appeared age appropriate.

As it turned out, and as it has turn out on a great many occasions since then, the students found nothing objectionable about the language restrictions. The ability to engage in and perform successfully is so surprising and reinforcing that the literary limitations seem immaterial. Examples of such reading material prepared for a variety of other students over the years were illustrated in earlier chapters. I am sad to say that examples of these early attempts are lost.

As mentioned in an earlier chapter, this stage is transitional until the fund of recognized words is increased sufficiently to engage in reading trade books, basals, high interest low vocabulary books or whatever else the student may like to read. The idea is to give them sufficient reading skill so that reading can become a regular activity that becomes the self generator of reading achievement. To get to this point, success has to be formally planned.

Self-Assessment

Testing is something that is usually done to students. However, students should be far more participant in their own assessment. Students need to be as specifically aware as possible of where they are and what and where they are going. Self-assessment helps the student be a more reflective, aware, and an engaged learner. Students should be active in monitoring their own progress and setting reasonable attainable goals. They can make good judgments about their own skills and learning if this is a regular part of all learning activities.

The notion of self-assessment may seem to contradict standard assessment practices. It may seem that students do not have the skill to assess their own instructional needs and progress. However, in the most important aspects of instructional activity, elementary age children are capable of handling many assessment activities. I was and advisor in a doctoral study (Kwang Seon Kim, 1991) in which Kim studied the ability of both regular students and students with learning disabilities to assess their own word knowledge. Elementary age student with and without learning disabilities are accurate in identifying which words they know or don't know on isolated word lists and in the context of reading selections. This is the most important skill required in identifying the appropriate instructional level reading material.

Students can tell for themselves when reading material is too hard to engage in with comprehension. They can learn to select much of their own independent and instructional level reading material. They can and should learn to inventory their skills and attainments. They should learn to check, compare to standards approximate, edit and revise; all these kinds of things are parts of assessment. They are also important parts of active and reflective learning.

Self-assessment as an integral part of instruction should be common practice. It is empowering to students. It is a useful tool in lifelong learning. Students should be engaged in monitoring their own progress, seeking helpful corrective feedback, and in deciding what to engage in next.

Appendix

HARGIS WORD LIST

Level 1

A an and away bad ball bed began big bike bit bite boy bug by can car cat caught climb day did do does dog down eat fell find fish food foot found fun gave girl go goes good got had happy has have he heard help her him his hit home house hurt I in is it knew know let like little look mad name no not of on one out play put ran ride rode run said sat saw see she snake some teeth the then think threw time to top tree tried up very want was water went wet what who will with woke yes you

Level 2

After again all animal apple are around ask at ate baby bat bear because begin bird black blue boat bought box break broke brown but buy call came cap catch cloth coat cold color come could cried cry cup dinosaur dirt door drive drop drove fall farm feet fire flew flower flyfor forest friend frog full funny game get ghost give glass green gun hat head held hill hold horse hot how hungry if jump kick knife lake leg lot loud love made make man me money monkey monster more mud my new now off old open orange picture pocket pole pond pull push rain red road rock sad say shoe sick sing sit sleep so soap stay stop stove swam swim take tall than their them there they thing thought throw too took toy tried truck try two ugly under wake walk were whale wheel when where white why win window wish woman wood work yellow zoo

Level 3

Almost am angry any arm as back barn be before behind being best birthday both bridge bump carry chair cook crawl cut draw drew each enough eye far farther fast father feel felt fight finger first from front grass hair hard here hook job just last left light long many may might morning mother mouth neck nest night now of or other our over part piece pour read rest roof room same sang scare sell shut side slow smell sold sound step table taste that these this those tie today together turn until us wash way we would write wrote your

Level 4

Able about air airplane alone also always another banana bank been better bottom brother bus bush cake candy Christmas class cloud cow crawl dark deep dish doctor dry duck ear either even every face fireman fix floor gas Halloween hammer high (ice cream) kitchen kitten less letter lion low men most much nail near next none nose nurse nut often only pack paint pan pants paper pen pencil people pet pick pie pink policeman pot puppy purple right ring rocket sa e second shark shirt short should sister soft sour spoon stick stream such sweet team thin three tiger toe tomorrow tooth towel train turtle warm which whose witch women word worm year yell

Level 5

Add alligator ambulance aunt bag bake became become belt bend beside best better bitter blanket blew blow body* bounce bread bring brought buffalo build built burn camp children chin circus clean clock close closet country cousin deer different divide dolphin earth edge elephant empty feather fork frighten fruit garage geese glad gloves foose gorilla grand grew grow hawk hour inch insect keep kept kill knee land leave lip mean met metal mile mine minute mittens month most motor mountain move multiple must near nearly neither ocean owl plastic point pretty pumpkin quick quiet ready remember rich river round rub sack sad sandwich self* shelf shiny shoot sign shoot sign since slid slide small soup spring square steal stole stomach strange street strong stuck subtract summer swing swung thick tiny tongue touch towel trouble uncle unless watch weather week weight while wide winter wipe wreck yesterday young yours

*Compounds formed with –thing, -body, -self, -one, and grand- are not listed but should be included. Regular forms ending with –s, -es, -ed, -ing, -er, and –est are not listed but should be considered a part of the lists.

REFERENCES

Allington, R. (2002). What I've learned about effective reading instruction. *Phi Delta Kappan, 85,* 740-747.

Ashlock, R. (2002). *Error patterns in computation: Using error patterns to improve instruction* (8th ed.). Upper Saddle River, New Jersey: Merrill Prentice Hall.

Betts, E. (1936). *The prevention and correction of reading difficulties.* Evanston: Row Peterson.

Betts, E. (1946). *Foundations of reading instruction.* New York: American Book Co.

Bond, G. & Dykstra, R. (1967/1997). The cooperative research program in first grade reading instruction. *Reading Research Quarterly, 2/32,* 1-142/348-427.

Buros, O. (2001). *The mental measurement yearbook* (14th ed.). Highland Park, New Jersey: Gryphon Press.

Carnine, D., Silbert, J., Kame'enui, E., &Tarver, S. (2004). *Direct instruction reading* (4th ed.). Upper Saddle River, New Jersey: Pearson Merrill Prentice Hall.

CEC Today (July-August-September 2004). New CEC policy on high stakes assessment. *CEC Today, 10,* 4.

Clymer, T. (1963/1996). The utility of phonics generalizations in the primary grades. *The Reading Teacher, 16/50,* 252-258/182-185.

Dolch, E. (1941). *Teaching primary reading.* Champaign: Garrard.

Durrell, D. (1969). Listening comprehension versus reading comprehension. *Journal of Reading, 12,* 455-460.

Fischer, S. (2001). *A history of writing.* London: Reaktion Books Ltd.

Forell, E. (1985). The case for conservative reader placement. *The Reading Teacher. 38,* 857-862.

Fry, E. (2002). Readability versus leveling. *The Reading Teacher, 56,* 286-291.

Gagne, R. (1970). Some new views of learning. *Phi Delta Kappan, 51,*468-472.

Gates, A. (1930). *Interest and ability in reading.* New York: Macmillan.

Gickling, E. & Thompson, V. (1985). A personal view of curriculum-based assessment, *Exceptional Children, 52,* 205-218.

159

Gickling, E., Hargis, C., & Alexander, D. (1981). The function of imagery in sight word recognition among retarded and nonretarded children. *Education and Training of the Mentally Retarded, 16*, 259-263.

Grimes, L., (1981). Learned helplessness and attribution theory: Redefining children's learning problems. *Learning Disabilities Quarterly, 4*, 91-100.

Hallahan, D. & Kauffman, J. (1986). *Exceptional Children* (3rd ed.). Englewood Cliffs: Prentice-Hall.

Hammill, D. (2004). What we know about correlates of reading. *Exceptional Children, 70*, 453-468.

Hargis, C. (2003). *Grades and grading practices: Obstacles to improving education and to helping at-risk students.* Springfield: Thomas.

Hargis, C. (1999). *Teaching and testing in reading: A practical guide for teachers and parents.* Springfield: Thomas.

Hargis, C. (1995). *Curriculum assessment: A primer* (2nd ed.). Springfield: Thomas.

Hargis, C. (1993). Success-based assessment. *Tennessee Educcation, 22*, 34-36.

Hargis, C., Terhaar-Yonkers, M., Williams, P., & Reed, M. (1988). Repetition requirements for word recognition. *Journal of Reading, 31*, 320-327.

Hargis, C. (1987). *Curriculum based assessment: A primer.* Springfield: Thomas.

Hargis, C. (1985, November). *Word introduction and repetition rates.* Paper presented at the 11th Southeastern IRA regional conference, Nashville, TN.

Hargis, C. (1982). *Teaching reading to handicapped children.* Denver: Love.

Hargis, C. (1978, July). *Word recognition development as a function of imagery level.* Paper presented at the summer meeting of the Linguistic Society of America, Champaign-Urbana.

Hargis, C., & Gickling, E. (1978). The function of imagery in word recognition development. *The Reading Teacher, 32*, 570-574.

Harris, A., & Sipay, E. (1975). *How to increase reading ability* (6th ed.). New York: David McKay.

Hatch, J. A. (2002). Accountability shovedown: Resisting the standards movement in early childhood education. *Phi Delta Kappan. 83*, 457-462.

Hewitt, F. & Taylor, F. (1980). *The emotionally disturbed child in the classroom: The orchestration of success* (2nd ed.). Boston: Allyn & Bacon.

Jacob, B. (2001). Implementing Standards: The California mathematics text-book debacle. *Phi Delta Kappan, 83*, 264-272.

Jansky, J. & de Hirsch, K. (1972). *Preventing reading failure: Prediction, diagnosis, intervention.* New York: Harper and Row.

Jenkins, J. & Pany, D. (1978). Standardized achievement tests: How useful for special education? *Exceptional Children, 44*, 448-453.

Johnston, F. (2002). Author's response. *The Reading Teacher, 56*, 215-216.

Kim, K. S. (1991). *A comparison study of learning disabled and regular students' ability to self-diagnose words using a computerized curriculum-based assessment system.* Unpublished doctoral dissertation, The University of Tennessee, Knoxville.

Loftus, E. & Suppes, P. (1972). Structural variables that determine problem-solving difficulty in computer-assisted instruction. *Journal of Educational Psychology, 63*, 531-542.

Mangieri, J. & Kahn, M. (1977). Is the Dolch list of 220 words irrelevant? *The Reading Teacher, 30*, 649-651.

Miller, G. (1956). The magical number seven, plus or minus two. *Psychological Review, 63*, 81-97.

Resnick, L. & Ford, W. (1981). *The psychology of mathematics for instruction.* Hillsdale: Lawrence Erlbaum.

Reys, R. (2001). Curricular controversy in the math wars: A battle without winners. *Phi Delta Kappan, 83*, 255-258.

Rosenshine, B. & Berliner, D. (1978). Academic engaged time. *British Journal of Teacher Education, 4*, 3-16.

Reutzel, D. & Cooter, R. (2004). *Teaching children to read: Putting the pieces together.* (4th ed.). Upper Saddle River, New Jersey: Pearson Merrill Prentice Hall.

Schemo, D. (June 10, 2004). Study finds senior exams are too basic. *New York Times/nytimes.com.*

Shearer, W. (1899). *The grading of schools.* New York: H. P. Smith Publishing Co.

Skinner, B. F. (1972). Teaching: The arrangement of contingencies under which something is taught. In N. G. Haring and A. H. Hayden (Eds.), *Improvement of instruction,* Seattle: Special Child.

Shinn, M. (Ed.). (1989). *Curriculum-based measurement: Assessing special children.* New York: The Guildford Press.

Smith, F. (2001). Just a matter of time. *Phi Delta Kappan, 82*, 572-576.

Smith, W. (1912). *All the children of all the people: A study of the attempt to educate everybody.* New York: Macmillan.

Spache, G. (1976). *Diagnosing and correcting reading disabilities.* Boston: Allyn and Bacon.

Stanovich, K. (1986). Matthew effects in reading: Some consequences of individual differences in the acquisition of literacy. *Reading Research Quarterly, 21*, 442-457.

Stiggins, R. (2002). Assessment crisis: The absence of assessment for learning. *Phi Delta Kappan, 85*, 758-765.

Thompson, V., Gickling, E., & Havertape, J. (1983). The effects of medication and curriculum on task-related behaviors of attention deficit disordered and low achieving peers. *Monographs in behavioral disorders: Severe behavior disorders of children and youth.* CCBD, Arizona State University. Series #6.

Trafton, P., Reys, B., & Wasman, D. (2001). Standards-based mathematics curriculum materials: A phrase in search of a definition. *Phi Delta Kappan, 83,* 259-264.

Tucker, J. (1985). Curriculum-based assessment: An introduction. *Exceptional Children, 52,* 199-204.

Reading Today (2004 February/March). Celebrate the Seussentennial. *Author, 21,* 21.

Zenger, W. & Zenger, S. (2002). Why teach certain material at specific grade levels? *Phi Delta Kappan, 84,* 212-214.

INDEX

A

Age appropriate material, 96, 97
Allington, R., 44, 48, 88
Alphabetic writing, 87, 88
Arithmetic assessment, 89-91
Ashlock, R., 91
Assessment for teaching, 29
Avoiding failure, 127, 128

B

Basal level, 47
Berliner, D., 48
Betts, E., 4, 29, 44, 73, 77, 151
Bond, G., 6
Buros, O., 82

C

Carnine, D., 33
Case histories, 27, 28
CEC Today, 124
Cerf, B., 108
Clymer, T., 87
Comprehension, 41, 76
    Listening, 36, 37
Cooperative Research Program in
    First-Grade Reading
    Instruction, 5, 6
Cooter, R., 33
Concreteness, 66-68
Council on Exceptional Children,
    124

Curricula, assigning of, 134
Curriculum-based measurement
    (CBM), 144-147
Curriculum casualties, 4, 6, 8
Curriculum rigidity, 4, 5
Curriculum, scope-and-sequence,
    22
Curriculum, seamless, 21

D

Decodable words, 54
Decoding, 54, 56
De Hirsch, K., 5
Diagnostic tests, 22, 116, 143
Diagnostic-prescriptive approach,
    121,122
Direct assessment, 95
Dolch, E., 51
Dolch Basic Sight Word List, 51
Double standard, 11, 12
Dr. Seuss, 53, 108
Drill, 61-68, 87
    (see also Repetition)
Durrell, D., 82
Dykstra, R., 6

E

Error patterns, 63, 90, 91

F

Failure, 12, 13, 16, 17, 28, 36

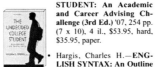